Joyful Witness

ISBN 0-9550771-0-9 (978-0-9550771-0-4)
Published by Kingcase Press
PO Box 8494
Prestwick
KA9 2WW

Text © Kathleen Bates 2005
Illustrations © Ronnie Russell 2005.

Printed by C & G Print, Troon KA10 6HR

Joyful Witness

Kathleen Bates

Illustrations by Ronnie Russell

Kingcase Press

This book is dedicated to all who read it,
in the hope that it may bring them comfort and cheer.

Contents

Oh, for the wonder that bubbles into my soul,
I would be a good fountain, a good well-head,
Would blur no whisper, spoil no expression.
(D.H. Lawrence: *Song of a man who has come through*)

But Mary kept all these things,
and pondered them in her heart.
(The Gospel according to St. Luke, 2, verse 19)

Chapter 1

Introduction

Coincidences: what do you think of them? Are they the products of mere chance? Or might they have a hidden *meaning*? You know the sort of thing: an unexpected meeting with the very person you need to meet; the arrival of a letter at an exceptionally appropriate time; two unusual but identical names or situations cropping up on the same day; the answer to a troubling question found in a book opened at random.

For over thirty years I have kept a record of coincidences such as these, coincidences which have happened in my ordinary family life. At first I kept my notebooks hidden at the bottom of a drawer, and refrained from talking too much about these precious experiences. Raised eyebrows and pitying indulgent smiles from adults, or alarmed expressions on the faces of my children, made me wary of referring to the unseen dimension which I sensed behind *visible* 'reality'. But sometimes, when a series of coincidences exploded into my life like fireworks suddenly lighting up the night sky, the joy and wonder were just too much to keep to myself! Gradually my family began to accept, then to share, my astonishment at the latest strange example of synchronicity. Nowadays they phone me to say 'I must tell you about a "Big C" that happened to me yesterday. It was amazing!'

Geoffrey Ashe, in his book *Miracles*, talks of

coincidences thus: 'Who knows? ... Trivial in themselves, they might, together, compose a continuing 'sign' of deep import, as a mass of dots composes a newspaper photograph.'

I personally feel that such coincidences are used as messages on some sort of higher wavelength to reassure us, comfort us - and ultimately lead us to God.

'Messages from whom?' asks the sceptic. 'Do you claim they come directly from God? Or maybe you think you have a guardian angel?'

I don't know. I don't claim to understand how the system works! I prefer to leave it *sine nomine* (without a name) and just feel a deep sense of gratitude for guidance received - or sometimes simply for a touch of humour which lightened a tense situation! But I do know from experience the truth of the late Archbishop William Temple's words: 'When I pray, coincidences happen.' It is to this truth that I want to testify, to *'bear witness'* - but in so doing I feel as if I am *'baring'* my very soul! To make public the contents of my private diaries, thereby revealing my inner thoughts is, perhaps, to run the risk of ridicule, just as if I were exposing my middle-aged body to public view. But the years which have brought physical changes have also brought with them the welcome benefit of *experience*, altering my attitude towards the phenomenon of coincidence.

Stress, depression, anguish, bereavement, loneliness - I have known all these. Yet how often, when difficult circumstances have made me feel like a lonely tightrope walker in a dark, cheerless place, I have suddenly, joyfully, become aware of an unseen network of help, like a golden safety net below me. I now believe - not because somebody has *told* me to believe, but because events in my own life have convinced me that it is so - that we are not left alone when we cry out for help; that God does answer when we call out in anguish, 'Oh God, please help me!' or even 'Oh God - *if you exist* - please help me!'

Again and again I have noticed, then noted in my diary, that coincidences have followed when I have earnestly, sometimes *desperately*, prayed for help. How well I remember one such time when, after a series of helpful coincidences, I was walking my dog beside a quiet pond in the local park. Suddenly I realised with joy that it is true what Jesus said - *'Ask and you shall receive; seek and you shall find; knock and the door shall be opened to you.'*

Of course, the door in question was not always the one I thought would be opened! Sometimes it was case of 'One door closes and another door opens' - the closed door being a disappointment, a major set-back of some kind, or even a bereavement. But as I continued to pray for guidance, through the darkness a light would appear, as if through an opening door - bringing consolation, reassurance, encouragement, reinforcement, new opportunities, practical help.

But of what use is a personal testimony like mine? How well I know the usual judgements!

– In this twenty-first century, with all our knowledge and modern technology, surely it is childish / unscientific / just plain crazy to listen to boring Christians babbling on about prayer and about what Jesus said two thousand years ago?

– What's all this about coincidences, visions, funny feelings and unseen dimensions? That's surely dabbling in dangerous waters. Call yourself a Christian? You should stick to the Scriptures!

– Why should I want to read about *your* experiences when plenty of interesting events have taken place in my own life? Coincidences happen. So what?

– You've been working too hard again. Take an aspirin and go and lie down!

Well, despite these and other objections, I *still* want to stand up and bear witness to the coincidences and other ways in which I have gradually been made aware of the unseen, timeless dimension beyond the commonplace of everyday living, and to the help I have received in answer to prayer. However, I do understand the viewpoint of the person who once said, 'If you say you have a revelation, I must have one too before I can believe you.'

So, yes, it is up to *you* to weigh up my testimony and judge whether or not you find it admissible evidence. But as you do so, look back on your own past experience, and reflect on any coincidence which has startled or amazed you. Did it perhaps occur at a time when you needed encouragement or consolation? Or maybe it just afforded you a smile when you were feeling low? Can you remember any time when (whether or not you have any religious belief) you uttered a fervent prayer - which was then answered in a remarkable way? Whatever your verdict on these matters, I hope that by bearing witness I may heighten your awareness of past, present and future coincidences, and - more importantly - that you will be encouraged, whenever you have a problem, to 'take it to the Lord in prayer' and to give thanks for blessings received.

Chapter 2

The Mysterious Ellipse

In my study, under my chair where I sit typing this, there is a warm attractive rug, a present from my daughter Linda. The design has a central white circle overlapped to left and right by a blue semi-circle. Each overlap produces a grey ellipse, like a pointed oval. This has proved to be a valuable visual aid in my attempt to define just how I feel when experiencing yet another striking coincidence. *Wherever* I happen to be at that moment, I usually stop in my tracks and keep very still, feeling that I am standing in the middle of just such an ellipse, where two completely different realities overlap - the one being at a precise point in our familiar measurable time-scheme, e.g. 7pm on Sunday 18 April, the other the unknown, but very real, time-*less* dimension, which I can only dimly apprehend, but which through experience I have come to sense and recognise.

My typical response on such occasions is to think, as I stand there with my jaw dropping in amazement at this latest coincidence, 'Ah, I *see*!' - in the sense of 'Ah, now I understand!' But what exactly *do* I understand as I stand there motionless, in astonished reaction to yet another postcard or letter or TV programme or tune or talk on the radio which coincides exactly - *at just the right time* - with some matter which has been preoccupying me? Above all, I experience an overwhelming sense of awe, an awareness of how very little I understand of the workings of this unseen dimension, which operates in some way that is far beyond our human 'logical' thought-pattern of cause and effect. How tiny a place I occupy in this immense invisible network which apparently links us all!

Usually such striking coincidences occur only occasionally, one at a time, but there have been memorable 'cluster days' when several have followed closely one after the other, leaving me gasping by evening!

On the other hand, one of the following chapters describes a series of coincidences which took place years apart, but which I instantly recognised as being linked by the same theme. (See *The Library Angel.*)

Also included in this testimony are two accounts of a different type. (*Winged Comfort, The Joyful Reunion*). These concern two very unusual experiences which, although they did not involve coincidence, nevertheless gave me the strong impression that I was within that mysterious ellipse where another, completely different, dimension overlaps our familiar ones of time and space.

At a conference on Science, Spirituality and Religion, I mentioned 'my' ellipse to one of the speakers.

'Ah!' he exclaimed, 'you have discovered the secret of your own mandala.'

Being unfamiliar with this term, I looked it up later in

my dictionary and found the following two definitions:

Mandala: 1. *(Hindu and Buddhist art) any of various designs symbolising the universe, usually circular.*

2. *(Psychology) such a symbol expressing a person's striving for unity of the self. (Sanskrit: circle).*

The second does indeed apply to 'my' ellipse, this precious symbolic shape which has proved so useful to me, by *uniting* two dimensions of reality, the seen and the unseen, the temporal and the timeless.

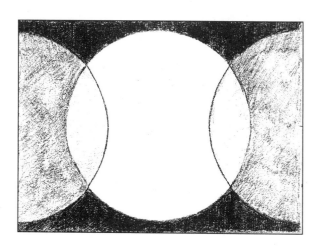

Chapter 3

The Question and the Answer

'I have a question for you,' I said to the man across the room from me, the man I knew would marry one day, even although he had not yet proposed.

'Well?' asked Bob with a smile, as he sat on the floor beside the glowing coal fire. The question had just popped suddenly into my head, in the same strange way as that certainty, on our first date two weeks previously, that this was my future husband.

A question! One question! What an understatement. There were so many things I did not know about this thirty-year-old man, six years my senior, who taught English at the school where I was a new teacher of French and German. We had first started to converse outside the staff room door, where my storage cupboard was located. When he had suggested that we go out for dinner one weekend I had hesitated, saying 'Not on Saturday. That's when I go out with Stanley.'

Stanley had been my first sweetheart, and since school days we had spent Saturday evenings together. All my friends assumed that we would become engaged. Gradually I had realised, however, that this relationship would never lead to marriage, and I smilingly changed the subject whenever the girls teased me about it. Now our Saturdays had become little more than a pleasant routine, a few hours of relaxation at the end of each week's hard work in the classroom.

Friday 29 November, then, had been the agreed rendez-vous with Bob: dinner at Ayr Station Hotel - an appropriate venue, for as the evening progressed I became uncannily aware that I had found a new 'travelling companion' with whom I was about to set off on a completely new 'journey'!

Up until then I had always scoffed at the idea of instant recognition of one's life-partner. I knew little about Bob. We had never held hands nor exchanged a kiss, and (in those pre-Pill days) had certainly never slept together. I had not even seen him often enough to be able to visualise his face in detail when we were apart. And yet, as we talked over dinner about our different experiences at Glasgow University and about music, poetry, religion, teaching, there had simply been no doubt in my mind that we would marry. Almost against my better judgement, I had found myself remembering lines from a Rodgers and Hammerstein song:

> *... And somehow you'll know, you'll know even then*
> *That somewhere you'll see her again and again.*
> *Who can explain it? Who can tell you why?*
> *Fools give you reasons; wise men never try.*

These words may seem sloppy and sentimental, but to me that evening they were quite the reverse. They expressed my new strange detached, wholly *objective* conviction that somehow our marriage had been arranged, that somewhere, on another unseen dimension, our future path had already been mapped out. Strong physical attraction, love and devotion would follow, but first and foremost those first hours together had been (for me at least!) an encounter on a deeply spiritual level, bringing with it a new awe-struck awareness of invisible guidance.

When on my return home my parents sleepily called out, 'How was your evening?' I had replied, 'Well, I've found my Parlicoot!', referring to a favourite childhood story about a little creature who travelled all alone through the forest until at last he found another Parlicoot to be his mate.

By the next morning, however, I began to have my doubts. Could I really trust these strange new thoughts? Surely reason demanded more circumspection, a little prudence? After all, my mind had been disciplined at university to arrange my ideas in logical order, to consider a question from different angles before reaching a measured conclusion. Perhaps this overwhelming attraction was just hormonal activity, caused by my biological clock?

Several of my friends had recently married. Had this triggered a sudden desire to follow their example? I recalled my solitary walk home after the most recent wedding. Thinking of the young couple's radiant happiness, I had found myself silently praying, 'Dear God, why does nobody want to marry me? I would love to make somebody happy like that!' With tears in my eyes, I had ruefully thought of a popular radio quiz master's description of each unmarried female contestant as 'an unclaimed treasure!' Perhaps this was to be my fate ...

Now I gave myself a shake. All such foolish thoughts

must be strenuously resisted. After all, I was only twenty-four! I had witnessed the misery of a friend who had rushed blindly into marriage because of peer-group pressure. Another, who had married at eighteen, was tied to the house with three children. No, I had other plans for my own future. Student life abroad - a year in France, five months in Germany - had given me a taste for travel and for using the languages I had studied. I was still young and energetic; the world was my oyster; life was full of exciting possibilities. Once I had completed my two years as a probationary teacher and repaid my parents at least in some measure for the financial sacrifices they had made for me, I would try to find work in Germany.

Again and again over the past two weeks I had weighed this argument against the persistent certainty that Bob and I belonged together. Now as I looked at this relatively unknown man comfortably ensconced beside the fire, I could scarcely believe what was happening. My mind was in turmoil. Totally confused, I wished that I could have some guidance.

Suddenly with great clarity, a memory flashed into my mind - a scene from my university days, though nothing to do with any of the subjects I had studied there. I remembered walking down University Avenue one crisp sunny day, past the circular 1930's-style Reading Room. As I passed in front of the next building, the neo-classical Wellington Church, something had made me stop in my tracks. My gaze fell upon the dark solid pillars of the church's façade, between which the cloudless blue sky glowed, luminous, endless. Transfixed by its beauty, I felt intensely aware of the striking contrast between the hard grey stone pillars and the infinity of space beyond them. A strange sadness, too vague to identify precisely, came over me. The architectural style of the building represented a civilisation which had passed away - and so, by association, the transience of human life and achievement; as a church it symbolised human yearning for a relationship with God; the tangible mass of these pillars appeared reassuring - but through time even hard stone crumbles away; the intangible sky, by contrast, was unchanging, eternal .... For some unknown reason tears came into my eyes as I stood there, and I had thought of Tennyson's lines.

Tears, idle tears, I know not what they mean,

Tears from the depth of some divine despair,

Rise in the heart and gather in the eyes ...

Somehow, inexplicably, this sadness had seemed almost like a kind of homesickness.

What did Bob remember from his University days? I wondered. Perhaps the inspiring English lectures by Professor Peter Alexander? The encouragement he had received from senior lecturer Hannah Buchan? Debates in the Students' Union? The pawnbroker's where he used to pawn his watch when short of cash?

'Here's the question,' I said, adopting a brisk tone of voice. 'Without stopping to think, what's the first scene that comes into your mind's eye when you think of your four years at University? Quickly! Tell me what you see. Don't stop to mull it over!'

'The very first thing, you say? Well, strange as it may

seem, what I'm remembering right now is one evening at sunset when I'd stepped out of the Reading Room for a cigarette. I looked over to Wellington Church, and between the pillars of the façade the cloudless sky was so magnificent that I stood stock still, almost hypnotised by its beauty'.

Amazed and awe-struck, I stared at him. Coincidence? Telepathy? Whatever the explanation, Bob and I were undoubtedly 'on the same wave-length'. Here was the confirmation I had been looking for. When, two weeks later, he proposed, I accepted; we were married the following June.

Now, forty years later, my abiding memory of that remarkable evening is not only that I found my future husband - but also that simultaneously I discovered a whole new *intuitive* way of experiencing life.

Chapter 4

Rebirth

'I'm sorry to tell you that Tom has just died'.

My mother, sitting in the armchair on my right, was desperately clutching the telephone, as if it were a lifeline, while she imparted the bad news to one relative after another. On my left, my father ....

Back home from the Sunday evening church service, he had sat down for a cup of tea, leaving the car on the road outside, with the intention of driving my sister to the railway station to catch the London train - but, alas, this time it was *he* who had had to leave us ... Just when he was about to tell our mother a piece of local news, he had given a gasp - and simply died, of a sudden massive heart attack.

It seemed to me, as I gazed in fearful awe at the pale, still presence of Death on that beloved face, that a terrible subtraction sum had been made. There in his favourite chair was his body - but minus his spirit. This body, familiar as it was, was not my Dad; it was meaningless without his personality, his *essence*. Where was his spirit now? That I could no longer communicate with him felt like torture. In the midst of my shock and grief a strange, unfamiliar worry tormented me. Did he know that he had now passed on? Was there anyone there to receive him, to comfort him? His mother, my Gran, for example?

Totally unprepared for the traumatic suddenness of this parting, I did not know how to react. My first thoughts were for my mother. For her sake I steeled myself to be strong and capable. On the funeral day and for the next two months, I struggled to maintain an air of calm composure, while inwardly I battled with the huge questions which now confronted me:

Does the spirit exist independently of the body?

If so, what happens after death?

Where does the spirit go?

Will we meet our loved ones again some day?

Where is God in all of this?

At home I tried to appear cheerful and normal for the sake of Bob and our two small daughters, not allowing myself to shed a single tear - but all the while the little girl inside me was silently sobbing, 'Oh, Daddy .... Daddy!'

The violence of this bottled-up grief frightened and confused me. Everyone else, I realised, must think me very lucky. And, indeed, so I was. I had a caring husband whom I loved dearly, two delightful children, a comfortable home in a quiet, pleasant part of town. When I looked in the mirror, I saw the same image as before - but in reality everything inside me had now totally changed. I felt completely isolated, trapped in some ghastly goldfish bowl which was preventing me from reaching any of my beloved family and friends.

All this was difficult enough to cope with. But

something even more mind-blowing was to follow ....

One night, about six weeks after the funeral, Bob and I had just snuggled down in bed together when we were startled by a loud thud at our front door.

'Surely that's somebody trying to break in!' we exclaimed, starting up in alarm. But what burglar would make such a loud noise? It sounded as if he had made a rush at the door, heaving at it with his shoulder in order to force it open. Hastily we reached for our clothes. I was trembling with apprehension.

But suddenly something strange happened. A wonderful sense of peace and reassurance enveloped both of us simultaneously. We stared at each other in puzzlement. Somehow we knew that there was nothing to worry about. We continued dressing, but now less hurriedly, then made our way calmly to the front door. There was not the slightest sign of any unwelcome visitor, nor any trace of damage to the door. Both garden and street were silent, deserted. And yet we had *both* heard that sudden loud noise, just before the strange calm had descended upon us!

Whatever could it all mean? Troubled, I began to wonder if maybe, just maybe, it could possibly have been my father, trying to reassure us that all was well with him? That thud on the front door was the sound which, in the month before his death, had announced his arrival. Because the newly-painted door had tended to stick, he would thud his shoulder against it and give it a strong shove, in order to open it.

A few mornings later, my mother telephoned me, in a state of considerable agitation.

'You'll have to contact the police for me,' she said urgently. 'Last night an intruder was at the back door, ringing the doorbell.'

I felt my hair stand on end. Being of a nervous disposition, my mother had been in the habit of barricading herself in whenever Dad was out at night. Both front and back doors had a lock, bolts and a chain. There were two doorbells, which sounded quite different from each other. This, too, was a safety precaution. In this way she could tell whether the caller was a stranger at the front door or my father, who always used the back door, after parking the car in the garage at the rear of the house. *He was the only person who ever used the back doorbell.* All other visitors used the front one.

Now I faced a dilemma. What was I to do? Phone the police, as my mother requested - but tell them what, exactly? I tried to convince her that she had only been dreaming, that perhaps on a subconscious level it had been wishful thinking on her part when she heard the back doorbell. But then the same thing happened two nights later, and she became even more alarmed. Remembering that she had always steered clear of any talk of a possible after-life, I could not risk frightening her by suggesting that these might have been paranormal experiences. That would have been too unkind, especially now that she was all alone at night. All I could do was keep telling her soothingly that the shock of my father's sudden death was doubtless producing unpleasant after-effects which would surely soon pass.

Meanwhile I myself felt close to breaking-point. Day and night I battled with huge questions concerning life and death, until I was in a state of total nervous exhaustion. To my shock and grief had now been added the primitive fear of an invisible dimension of spirit!

Realising that I desperately needed to give expression to these overpowering emotions, I turned to my well-thumbed books of English poetry. Many poets, I knew, had channelled the grief of loss and bereavement into exquisite poems, some of which I already knew by heart. In particular, I recalled two lines from Milton's *Paradise Lost:*

'The mind is its own place, and in it self
Can make a Heav'n of Hell, a Hell of Heav'n.'

How true! But how was I to escape from my own present Hell? Finally admitting to myself that I needed help, I made an appointment for a private talk with my parish minister, a lovely, caring pastor. Surely he, who so often spoke of the Resurrection, would be able to shed light on my confusion regarding the recent noises in the night? But when I poured out the whole story to him he could only shake his head sadly, saying, 'I'm afraid I can't help you there, Kath. What you need, I think, is professional medical help.'

I sensed that he was extremely wary of being drawn into anything which might be classed as Spiritualism. But then, so was I! Remembering how older people often warned the young about 'dabbling' in séances, I thought of Bob's account of his own terrifying experience with a ouija board when he was a student. (On that occasion the upturned glass had spelled out a name, then shot off the table and smashed itself against a wall. The following week a friend of that same name was killed in a road accident.) I certainly did not want to try to conjure up any spirits of the dead. If there was, in fact, life after death, this would apply to evil people as well as good, and I could easily understand the dangers involved in any attempt at making contact.

But ... But what if the attempt at contact were the other way round? If someone 'on the other side' had been trying to contact me? How was I to cope with this totally new situation, *completely unsolicited on my part*? Who could help me? Who could advise me? For the sake of Bob and the children, I somehow had to pull myself together, but I desperately needed to talk with someone who had been through the same situation. I felt as if I were in a tiny boat, trying to steer a straight course in a vast, uncharted ocean.

Bob, perplexed and anxious, suggested that perhaps the only course of action left to us was a visit to the local Spiritualist meeting-place. In order to help me, he was prepared to overcome his misgivings about séances. As for myself, I was not at all happy at the idea.

'Dad never had any truck with Spiritualism', I remember thinking. 'Surely I don't have to go there to find help?'

Yet where else could I go? Life after death seemed to be a taboo subject of conversation, one which would likely be, at the very least, embarrassing to my friends or, more probably, lead them to suspect that I was mentally deranged. Perhaps, when he urged me to see my doctor, the minister had thought that the whole story had been a figment of my over-wrought imagination. Maybe that would have been my conclusion also - *had not Bob simultaneously had the same experience.*

We agreed that the apparently paranormal occurrence had not seemed at all *evil*. Although the initial thud at the door had been alarming, our lasting impression was one of peace and loving reassurance. If this had been a message of love from my father, how could I turn away and refuse to accept it?

Faced with no alternative (as it seemed), we plucked up courage one Sunday evening and went along to the Spiritualists' meeting. There we received a kindly welcome, but when I was told that someone who had suddenly 'passed over' wanted to reassure me that all was well with him, this message, through a third party, meant very little to me. It might, or might not, have been from my father.

I could understand and sympathise with mourners - especially bereaved parents - who longed for contact with their departed loved ones. I could believe that some people had natural psychic ability, just as others had the gift of perfect pitch. I could see that these local Spiritualists had the laudable aim of comforting the broken-hearted. But somehow, as far as I was concerned, this evening had merely served to confirm that the Spiritualist church was not for me. Not only did I still have my instinctive wariness about séances, but I also now felt that Spiritualism was too earth-bound. Its parameters were too limited. It seemed too human-centred, rather than *God-centred*.

Since early childhood I had taught to say my prayers at bedtime, and to attend church every Sunday. As I grew up I had come to cherish the interior of a church - any church - as a precious sanctuary, a place where I could find peace, and experience a sense of the numinous, of the mystery and wonder of God's presence in the midst of the noisy hustle and bustle of life. And over the years I had acquired the habit of 'taking everything to God in prayer', to quote the old hymn. All my everyday concerns: my teenage angst, my pre-exam nerves, my longing for a loving partner, my challenges as a teacher, my joys and hopes as a wife and mother - all these I had taken to God each night, thanking Him for blessings received, then asking for forgiveness, help, guidance, strength. But now, how was I to pray?

How I longed to worship God as before! But how could I, when feeling guilty about my preoccupation with that psychic experience - something which I had been taught to regard as forbidden fruit, something which frightened me? For I was scared to admit the possibility of an unseen dimension outwith my control. When that inexplicable feeling of peace had descended on Bob and me, I had instinctively, intuitively, connected it with my father. But the very thought that the dead could return to communicate with the living, and the idea that my everyday actions might be observed by someone invisible - however loving and benevolent - filled me with alarm.

What confusion! Surely there must be someone, somewhere who could give me advice, and help me regain my equilibrium? But who? Where? I was becoming desperate, more and more distressed at my inability to 're-connect' with God, to whom I had previously taken all my worries and concerns. Now I could identify with the writer of Psalm 42:

As a hind longs for the running streams, so do I long for thee, O God. With my whole being I thirst for God, the living God. When shall I come to God and appear in his presence? Day and night tears are my food; 'Where is your God?' they ask me all day long. As I pour out my soul in distress, I call to mind how I marched in the ranks of the great to the house of God, among exultant shouts of praise, the clamour of the pilgrims.

All I felt I could do was try to follow the Psalmist's example, given in his next five lines, which are then used as a sort of chorus:

How deep I am sunk in misery, groaning in my distress; Yet I will wait for God; I will praise him continually, my deliverer, my God.

Finally (no doubt to my family's relief) I admitted defeat, and went to my doctor for help. He prescribed tranquillisers, and arranged for me to have some counselling. The pills helped me to feel calmer during the day and to sleep at night. Gradually regaining a sense of equilibrium, I established a pattern for each evening: a warm milky drink, a good book, and the evening prayer from a book of daily prayers. My favourite was William Barclay's *The Plain Man's Book of Prayers*. This consisted of a morning prayer, an evening prayer and a Bible reading for each day of the month. The very act of recalling the day's date and looking up the appropriate page constituted a step on the road to recovery. At the time of my darkest despair I had neither known nor cared to know which day of the month we were at.

As for the counsellor, it very quickly became apparent that he had no more idea than I had of the answers to the questions which had been troubling me. For him, there was absolutely no need to believe in the existence of God. That I felt such a need, he explained, was only because I had '*a dependent personality*'. This summary dismissal of my faith made me so indignant that I decided not to go back to him - and in making that decision, I suddenly realised that I was now feeling stronger, more able to cope: in short, more *independent* of him!

I worked out a kind of practical code of conduct for myself, which I called 'All the A's': I had to *acknowledge* all the recent traumatic events, *accept* them (not easy, but necessary), - at the same time *accepting* that there were some questions to which I would not, could not, as yet know the answers, - then *act accordingly*, continue with my everyday life as before, *assimilating* this new *awareness* as best I could. Gratefully, I remembered a quotation from Paul's first letter to the Corinthians (chapter 13, verse 12), words which my Sunday School teacher had once asked us to memorise:

For now we see through a glass darkly; but then face to face: now I know in part; but then shall I know even as also I am known.

One morning I was in the back garden, hanging out the washing, when suddenly, inexplicably, a wonderful thought came to me, filling me with joy: I could now *believe* the story of Jesus' resurrection! Not because a preacher in a pulpit had told me to, not because it formed part of the 'package' presented to dutiful members of Christian churches, but because of *my own experience.*

Recalling the thud at our front door and the ringing of my mother's back doorbell, both typical signs of my father's arrival, I remembered how, it had been a *typical* action on the part of Jesus which had enabled two of his disciples to recognise him after his death. Mourning for him, they did not grasp the amazing fact that he had risen from the dead, until they saw him breaking the bread and offering it to them, in exactly the same way as he had done in the past. (Luke 24, verses 30, 31). It dawned on me with joy that, at long last, I had found someone - Jesus Christ - who understood about life after death! Full of relief and gladness, I resolved to re-read the Gospels (the 'Good News') in this new light, knowing that Jesus had often told his friends that after his crucifixion he would rise again and come back to them.

A little while and you see me no more; again a little while and you will see me ... then you will be joyful, and no one shall rob you of your joy. (John 16, verse 16,22).

Over the next few days I pored eagerly over the New Testament. I noted that in the story of the rich man and Lazarus, (Luke 16, verses 19-31), Jesus had included the possibility of someone returning from the dead. He had not said that this was impossible or that it was evil, but had simply emphasised that such a *psychic* event was not of any *spiritual* value. The way of spiritual progress through life was the observation of the great commandments, which were summed up in these words:

Love the Lord your God with all your heart, with all your soul, with all your mind and with all your strength. Love your neighbour as yourself. (Mark 12, verses 28-34).

Neither academic study nor intellectual argument was required in order to be part of God's kingdom; all that was required was a child-like faith in God as Father.

I tell you, whoever does not accept the kingdom of God like a child will never enter it. (Mark 10, verse 15).

My desperate need of God, my 'dependent personality', was not a negative trait but a positive asset!

How blest are those who know their need of God; the kingdom of Heaven is theirs. (Matthew 5, verse 3).

The stability which I craved was offered here:

What then of the man who hears these words of mine and acts upon them? He is like a man who had the sense to build his house on rock. The rain came down, the floods rose, the wind blew, and beat upon that house; but it did not fall, because its foundations were on rock.
(Matthew 7, verses 24, 25).

What now interested me was what Jesus said to his disciples when he appeared to them after his death. He promised them the Holy Spirit - that is, the God-given power to carry out his instructions. These were to proclaim repentance which brings the forgiveness of sins, and to heal the sick.

'Begin from Jerusalem,' he said. *'It is you who are the witnesses to it all. And mark this: I am sending upon you my Father's promised gift; so stay here in this city until you are armed with the power from above.'*
(Luke 24, verses 48, 49).

'Begin from Jerusalem'. What courage that required! All over that city, the people who had put Jesus to death would doubtless be on the lookout for his disciples, determined to get rid of them too, so that all traces of Jesus' teaching would be stamped out and forgotten. His followers hid themselves away behind closed doors.

And then came the wonderful Change! Just over six weeks after the Crucifixion, the disciples were all together in one room, when suddenly they felt as if they had been set alight. They had a collective vision of flames descending upon each one of them, filling them with courage and power. They found, too, that they were able to speak in foreign languages, thus possessing the necessary means of spreading the Gospel, both immediately, to the foreigners in Jerusalem and, later, to the people of other lands. Now they knew and understood what Jesus had meant when he promised them the Holy Spirit.

The Holy Spirit - or, as it is often called, the Holy *Ghost.* As I pored over the marvellous story of Pentecost in Chapter 2 of the Acts of the Apostles, I thought of this other name, which is often used at the end of prayers: 'In the name of the Father, the Son and the Holy Ghost'. According to a German lecturer at my teacher training college, this was the Germanic alternative to the Latin *Spiritus Sanctus*. It originated in the 8th century, when Anglo-Saxon missionaries were attempting to convert the fierce Germanic tribes to Christianity. The most notable of these missionaries was St Boniface, later to become the patron saint of Germany. He was accorded the name Boniface by the Pope, presumably because of all his good works, but his real name was Wynfryth. (I paid special attention to this, because, *coincidentally*, I had once had a brief romance in Freiburg with a young German student called Winfried!) Wynfryth knew that the Northern Europeans had a great fear of the long winter darkness and of returning spirits of the dead. He assured them that the Holy Ghost (*der Heilige Geist*), which Jesus had promised his followers, was more powerful than any of *their* ghosts. As Christians, they would be fully protected from evil spirits. Legend has it that Wynfryth demonstrated this power by cutting down a sacred oak in a sacred grove. Filled with superhuman strength, he struck it with his axe, and the mighty tree toppled over, to the terror of the watching Druids. They were convinced that Thor would instantly avenge such sacrilege, but when nothing happened, they fell to their knees, converted by the superior power of the Christians' God.

Now, twelve centuries later, I too was strengthened by the thought of the power of the Holy Ghost, as I struggled to acknowledge, accept and assimilate my awareness of an unseen dimension, the knowledge that 'there is more to life than meets the eye'. The Lord's Prayer, which Jesus taught his disciples, took on a fresh, more profound meaning for me, especially the words: *'Deliver us from evil'* and 'Thine *is the kingdom, the power and the glory'*.

I established the habit of repeating it every morning and every night - a habit which has lasted more than thirty years. It was from this time onward that I began to notice more and more coincidences, to note them in my special diary, and to ponder over them with awe and wonder.

Thus, feeling protected, comforted and strengthened, I gradually emerged - as if reborn! - from the darkness of the 'valley of the shadow of death' into a new, joyful life of deeper faith and trust in God.

Chapter 5

The Library Angel

There is a book in my study which I hesitate to open, so connected in my mind as it is with death. Strange as this may seem, however, I would never willingly part with it, because it is precious to me in a special way. For this book was the first of many to which I feel I have been led, in order to make me aware of another dimension beyond the visible, beyond this material, materialistic world of ours. It represents my first startling encounter with what the late Arthur Koestler called 'the Library Angel': the phenomenon of being directed, without knowing why, to a certain book or newspaper article, where you find a passage or phrase (or even a single word) which you had been trying to remember, or which gives you much-needed guidance and the deeply comforting impression that you are not, after all, quite alone at a time of crisis. Help is at hand!

Homeward-bound one Friday afternoon, I was sitting in a train, eagerly perusing a book of German poetry. A final year student of French and German at Glasgow University, I was pleased to have found this collection, not only because it contained many of my favourite poems, but also because the English translation at the bottom of each page afforded me easy access to those which I did not yet know. Another benefit was practice in German-English translation, to prepare me for my forthcoming final examinations. Did I agree with the translator's rendering of the poet's intentions? I asked myself as I pored over Hugo von Hofannthal's *Terzinen über Vergänglichkeit (Three-line Stanzas on Transience)*. Suddenly the ideas behind the words were impressed upon me so strongly that I had to put the book down in order to think them through. In particular, the end of the poem, with the final three-line stanza followed by the emphatic single line, struck me with unusual force:

> *Dann: dass ich auch vor hundert Jahren war*
>
> *Und meine Ahnen, die im Totenhemd,*
>
> *Mit mir verwandt sind wie mein eignes Haar,*
>
> *So eins mit mir als wie mein eignes Haar.*

(And then - that I was also in existence a hundred years ago and my forebears in their shrouds are as related to me as my own hair is, are as much part of me as my own hair.)

I thought of the physical traits I had inherited from my father's side of the family: brown eyes, brown hair, short stature, a tendency to plumpness, whereas my slim sister had inherited our mother's figure and her blue eyes. In particular, my paternal grandmother, my beloved Gran, sprang to mind. The eldest of eleven children, she had been forced to leave school at the age of twelve because her help was needed at home. Although she had never, therefore, had any opportunity for higher education, she and I had a special relationship, which had been precious to me since my earliest childhood. How often she had 'kissed me better', holding me close to her plump comforting bosom! How often I had been guided by her brisk common sense, so that even now, as a young adult,

I often asked myself in tricky situations, 'What would Gran do?' The closeness of our relationship was doubtless reinforced by our physical resemblance, and, as the train approached my station, I thought of the unknown ancestors from whom she, then my father, then myself, had inherited our short stature and our brown eyes. For how many hundreds of years had these genes been transmitted, and where had they originated?

When I got off the train, ready to walk the short distance to my home, I was surprised to see my father waiting with the car outside the station. 'I've come to meet you because I wanted to prepare you for a shock,' he said. 'Your Gran suffered a severe stroke yesterday, and now I think she's dying.'

In the course of that painful weekend, as I tried to help and comfort my dear Gran, holding a cup of water to her parched lips, stroking her forehead, clasping her hand, my priorities were changed for ever. How much less important my finals seemed now - even despite my great fear of failing, since the University regulations dictated that students had to wait ten years before being allowed to retake them. How much more important, how precious, were loving human relationships! *This* was what mattered in life, I decided, *this* was reality, *this* was security. All the intellectual challenges which I had found so stimulating and enjoyable at University suddenly seemed by comparison little more than mere bagatelles, froth on the surface of things, pastimes in an ivory tower. No doubt an over-reaction in my grief and distress, but even yet, several decades later, the values established that weekend have remained, determining my daily actions, with my desire to foster harmonious human relationships still outweighing my passionate loves of language and of music.

***

One morning in March eight years later, I received a letter, out of the blue, from the youngest of my Gran's ten brothers and sisters, my short, plump, brown-eyed Uncle Gavin. Knowing that I had studied German poetry, he sought my help in finding and translating the words of a German song which he had recently heard on his car radio. It was, he thought, one of Schubert's many *Lieder*, a musical setting of words by a German poet. He explained that he had of late attended so many friends' funerals that he had, as he put it, 'nearly worn out my funeral weeds'. Very depressing! - but this song had brought him comfort. He had missed the title, but just as he had switched on the radio, the presenter had been giving the translation: something along the lines of *Death comes as the cool of the evening after the long hot tiring day*.

Eager to help, I went to my local library, but could not trace any poem which spoke of death in this way. I wrote to the BBC and to the Royal Scottish Academy of Music and Drama but no reply was immediately forthcoming from either. My old university textbooks had been stored away since the birth of our two daughters. (I had given up my teaching job in order to care for them at home.) However, in my search for Uncle Gavin's poem, I was now enjoying re-reading my volume of *German Verse*.

Thus it was that, three weeks later, this book was once

again lying open at Hugo von Hofmannsthal's poem about the transience of human life, on the never-to-be-forgotten April evening, when my mother telephoned to say that my father had just died of a massive heart attack.

On his funeral day, a letter arrived from the RSAMD. The librarian said that she had been unable to find a Schubert setting of a poem about death coming as the cool of the evening, at sunset, after the long hot tiring day, but hoped the enclosed poem, which Schubert set to music in his song *Die Muttererde (Mother Earth)* was perhaps what my uncle had heard, since it began: *Des Lebens Tag (Life's day)*. I felt my hair stand on end as I read these words, so appropriate and so timely on that day of all days. In translation they read:

Life's day is oppressive and sultry,

The breath of Death light and cool,

It wafts us gently down,

Like withered leaves, into the quiet grave.

The moon shines and the dew falls

On the grave as on the flowery meadow;

So as our friends' tears fall down over it

They are illuminated by a gentle ray of hope.

All of us, both great and small,

Mother Earth gathers to herself;

O, if we but looked her straight in the face

We would not fear being taken to her bosom!

Seven years after Uncle Gavin's original request, an

astonishing coincidence occurred on the morning after *his* funeral. Unlike my father, Uncle Gavin had died not suddenly, but after months of cancer. All that summer we had had an enjoyable exchange of letters, mostly concerning our religious faith, and his courageous spirit had been an inspiration to me. He had retired to the island of Bute in the Firth of Clyde, and had not wished me to visit him, because he did not want anyone apart from doctors and nurses to see his emaciated body. At last his spirit was set free, and his funeral took place on 5 November.

The next morning, a Sunday, I returned home from church to find that someone had delivered the Church of Scotland magazine *Life and Work*. Stooping to pick it up from the mat, I saw that the front cover had a beautiful photograph of a sunset. For the first time that I could ever remember, a verse of a poem had been superimposed on the cover illustration, placed beside the title of the main article: *A True Dignity for the Dying*.

Once more I felt my scalp tingle as I realised that this verse was from the translation of a German poem! It was Eichendorff's *Im Abendrot. (At Sunset)*:

> *So wide, so still and deep the peace*
> *Spread round us in the evening glow*
> *Weary of all our wandering,*
> *We ask if death be so.*

Chapter 6

The Comforter

'Escape! We have to get away!'

This thought was uppermost in our minds as Bob and I waved goodbye to our three children one July evening. Behind them on the doorstep stood the reassuring figures of my sister and brother-in-law, who had travelled from Manchester to Ayrshire that afternoon in order to 'hold the fort' in our absence.

Illness and stress had taken their toll recently. Bob's recurrent bladder cancer had meant yet another operation; his elderly mother needed our constant support; both full-time teachers, we had had end-of-term reports to cope with as well as the daily demands of the classroom; June had brought extra family activities, enjoyable but tiring. The children had all needed ferrying to and fro: our son Michael to various sports events, our daughters, Sally and Linda, to rehearsals for their school's production of Gilbert and Sullivan's *H.M.S. Pinafore*. Now that the summer term was finally over we were totally exhausted - physically, mentally and spiritually.

Experience has taught me to hand everything over to God in such situations, so for the previous week I had prayed:

'Please, God, give us Your support - *and make us aware of it*. Please send us Your Holy Spirit to guide us, so that we can come back spiritually refreshed, certain that You are always present and know our every need. Through Jesus Christ our Lord, Amen.'

There is something exhilarating about setting off into the unknown, ready to go where the Spirit moves us! All Bob and I knew was that we felt drawn to making a little pilgrimage to the island of Iona where St Columba had settled and where, we had read, Heaven seems especially close, in the same mystical way as at Glastonbury and Chartres.

Because it would be teatime before my sister and her family could arrive from Manchester, we decided to travel only the short distance to Helensburgh. There we could pay a morning visit to the famous Hill House, designed by Charles Rennie Mackintosh, before continuing our journey north-westwards. To ensure a room for the night, I had made use of the Tourist Board's Book-a-Bed-Ahead service, and we set off gaily that sunny evening, looking forward to finding the address the Tourist Board had given us, where we hoped to enjoy a quiet carefree sleep and a leisurely breakfast.

Over supper at our Helensburgh guest-house, our chatty host asked us where we were going next.

'Oban tomorrow night, then somewhere on Mull for two nights, with a visit to Iona,' we said. 'Probably Tobermory. That's the only place we know of on Mull - where the galleon from the Spanish Armada sank in the bay.'

'Oh no!' exclaimed our host. 'Tobermory's at the wrong end of Mull for visiting Iona. Bunessan, on the south-west of the island, would be far better.'

So our itinerary was beginning to take shape! - the Hill House, Oban, Bunessan, Iona. However, the following morning I had a disappointment. At the Helensburgh Tourist Office, after booking overnight accommodation in Oban, I asked for directions to the Hill House.

'I'm afraid it's not open yet,' said the girl. 'Can you wait until this afternoon?'

No, we decided. We would rather set off immediately so that we could enjoy the beautiful scenery without having to worry about reaching Oban before nightfall. It was a pity, but we would just have to postpone our visit to the Hill House.

But isn't remarkable how often a source of disappointment - or indeed annoyance - turns out to be truly a blessing in disguise? It's as if God is giving us a nudge, saying, 'Pay close attention and see how this fits into what I have planned for you!'

'Yes, the Tobermory office has found you a place in Bunessan,' announced the Oban Tourist Office assistant the next morning. 'The Hill House has a double room free.'

The Hill House! Ting! I felt a sudden tingle of exhilaration in the certainty that this was no 'mere coincidence' but an unmistakable sign that the Holy Spirit was indeed present and leading us on our way, in both the physical sense and the spiritual.

What would the Hill House have in store for us? I wondered as the car ferry made its way westwards towards the mountainous island of Mull. As the mainland receded, all our recent problems seemed to melt away and I stood beside Bob, relaxed and happy, with just a tiny thrill of anticipation at the thought of a little mystery to solve!

From the ferry terminal at Craignure, we decided not to drive directly to Bunessan across the southern end of Mull but instead to head north to Tobermory. After a pleasant lunch overlooking the sunny bay, we set off on the longer, much wilder route round the rugged north coast of the island. Hundreds of sheep, scattered across the rough terrain, were roaming freely, often straying on to the narrow single-track road. Then the track turned south, following the indented coastline, and more than once my hair stood on end when, encountering another vehicle on a blind bend, Bob had to reverse the car several hundred yards to the nearest passing-place, while I nervously eyed the rocks far below at the foot of the cliffs. Up, up we climbed, past sunlit valleys, in and out of the grey mist of the clouds which concealed the mountain summits. Magnificent scenery! - but all the same I was relieved when we rejoined the main Craignure - Bunessan road! From this south side of Loch Scridain, a long sea-loch, we could see in the distance the lonely island of Staffa, where the sound of sea birds and Atlantic breakers in the spectacular Fingal's Cave inspired Mendelssohn to write his *Hebrides* Overture.

At last we reached the tiny village of Bunessan - but there was no sign of any Hill House. Bob stopped at the police station to enquire and was told that we had already passed it.

'Drive back for about a mile and you'll see a modern bungalow on the right behind a farm gate,' said the policeman. 'You can't miss it - it stands all on its own overlooking the loch.'

A light drizzle had begun to fall. Retracing our route,we soon caught sight of a huge gaily-coloured golf umbrella being waved at us above a farm-gate. Our host had been standing there on the lookout. Welcoming us, he took our suitcases and led the way into the Hill House.

The guest house, he told us, still had a few items belonging to his daughter, an art teacher. It was her room whenever she came back to visit her parents. On the dressing-table there were, indeed, two of her possessions: a framed group photograph and a large round painted pebble bearing her name, SALLY.

'Ah, there's a coincidence!' I exclaimed. 'Our daughter's name is also . . . '

My voice trailed away in total disbelief as I took a closer look at the photograph - the cast of Ayr Academy's recent production of *H.M.S. Pinafore*, with our two daughters, Sally and Linda, smiling out at us!

Utterly amazed, the three of us stood stock-still, gazing at the photograph and at one another. The powerful effect of this 'coincidence' was so overwhelming that any explanation would be inadequate. We could only stand there in awe and wonder, sensing the presence of some invisible power that had led us to this place. The information that the daughter had spent the summer term at Ayr Academy teaching art and helping back-stage with the opera did nothing to reduce our sense of wonder. It only added one more to all the elements of our special journey which had led us here to this experience: our late departure from home, our Helensburgh host telling us of Bunessan, the Hill House, the Book-a-Bed-Ahead service, through which complete strangers had found rooms for us in guest-houses which were totally unknown to us.

Even today, many years later, the memory of this moment of amazed recognition brings me strength and joy, renewing my faith in the ever-present Holy Spirit, the Holy Ghost, the Comforter.

Chapter 7

When Mother-in-law Came to Stay

'I can hardly manage the stairs any more'. Bob's mother's voice was faint and trembling. My fingers tightened on the telephone receiver as I realised that this was now a major emergency. The bathroom in her large old four-bedroom house was on the first floor. Since being widowed two years previously she had slowed down markedly and had recently been forced to use a walking stick. What if she fell as she tried to negotiate the stairs - especially at night? She lived over twenty miles away. Bob had no brothers or sisters; we were her only family, solely responsible for her welfare. There was no question about it: she would have to come and live here, so that we could look after her. But our little house already felt too small for the five of us. To build on a granny flat would take far too long. She needed help *now*.

'Try not to worry,' I told her, attempting to sound calm and reassuring. 'Tomorrow Bob and I will start looking for a nice little two or three-room house for you near here'.

Easier said than done! I knew that all the single-storey houses on our housing estate had at least five rooms. But surely there might be a smaller house in the adjacent older part of our suburb, the part which was formerly a country village? There was a combined post office and general store in its main street. If she had a little house nearby, she could manage a short walk to collect her pension and to buy any small items she needed. That would give her fresh air and exercise, whilst we would do her main weekly shopping at the supermarket.

But alas! No 'For Sale' signs were in evidence in the former village, and scrutiny of the local newspapers and of estate agents' windows yielded no results. What a dilemma! Would we be forced to move house ourselves? To give up our beloved home and lovely garden in this quiet cul-de-sac, where the children could play safely? To leave all our friendly neighbours?

'Please, God, show us what to do for the best,' I prayed every day. 'Over to You! I just don't know *what* to do.'

Two anxious weeks passed. Then, on a Saturday morning, collecting for a children's charity, I arrived on the doorstep of a friend who, I knew, was also house-hunting.

'Any luck yet? Have you found a bigger house with a granny flat for your parents?' I asked, and told her of our problem.

'Wait a minute!' exclaimed Betty. 'This very morning the postman brought the latest list of properties from the estate agent. I'm certain that there is a one-bedroom bungalow for sale near the post office. That's so unusual that I noticed it particularly.'

She fetched the list, and, sure enough, the property she pointed out looked exactly what we wanted. Having noted the estate agent's telephone number, I took to my heels and ran all the way home. Within twenty minutes I had spoken to both the estate agent and the owner of the bungalow, arranging to bring my mother-in-law to view it the next afternoon. By the following day we had made a verbal offer to the owners; by the end of the week our lawyers had confirmed the deal in writing and an entry date had been arranged.

How fervently I gave thanks for this answer to our prayers!

***

Three years later, however, my prayers had once again become prayers of supplication rather than of thanksgiving. It had become obvious that Bob's mother could no longer live on her own. One evening she had fallen and, unable to get up, had lain all night on the floor of her living-room. Parkinson's Disease had been diagnosed. We would have to take her in and look after her.

But even with the best will in the world, this was not going to be easy. For two years Bob had been suffering from cancer of the bladder. Every three months he had to have a hospital check-up; each time this had involved yet another minor operation to remove more cancer cells. Because his mother was given to bouts of depression, we had been trying to conceal his condition from her. As I visualised the forthcoming scenario, I wondered despairingly how I was going to manage. Sometimes Bob's urinary tract became blocked and I had to rush him to hospital in the middle of the night. I could just imagine his mother's alarm and despondency, which would sap my morale at the very time when Bob would need all my attention, love and support. It was already a daily struggle to keep cheerful and strong for his sake and for the children - in addition to coping with my full-time teaching job.

By now Sally was away at university, but with the two other teenage children still at home we would have to build an extension to our house in order to give Gran a proper room of her own. The builders we employed claimed to be specialists in house extensions, and the foundations of the new living-room and bathroom were quickly laid. But suddenly the firm was declared bankrupt, and all work stopped. In desperation we called in another building firm to finish the uncompleted jobs.

Meanwhile my mother-in-law had to be rushed to hospital for an emergency hernia operation. This was successful - but where could she convalesce? She could not live at home, and our house was still like a building site! Desperate enquiries eventually resulted in her being installed, confused and unhappy, in temporary accommodation in a home for the elderly, while we tried to hurry the new builders along.

At last the room which was to be hers was ready to be furnished. Although Bob was still in pain from his latest surgery, he and I spent the exceptionally rainy school autumn holiday week trailing round the town, choosing a carpet, curtains and other items which we hoped would please her, determined to have everything ready for her arrival the following weekend.

But, as Robert Burns put it: *The best-laid schemes o' mice and men gang aft agley!*

The night before she was due to move in, our central

heating system broke down. A plumber arrived in the morning, and at what was to have been the appointed hour of Gran's arrival he had the carpet rolled back and the floorboards up, making access to her new room possible only to somebody nimble enough to jump over the gaping hole. Bob spent a difficult afternoon trying to smooth his indignant mother's ruffled feathers, assuring her that yes, she was more than welcome to come and live with us, but that no, she couldn't come just yet ... Not a very auspicious start!

By ten o'clock that evening, however, she was at last installed in her room, sound asleep in her new bed. In our living-room were piled cardboard boxes containing her clothes and various objects of sentimental value. On top of the latter lay a tiny book entitled *Hervey's Meditations*, published in 1746. Chuckling appreciatively over the elegance of the eighteenth-century prose, I decided that this would make a welcome 'change of ideas' - as the French say - after our stressful day, and took the little book off to bed with me. Knowing that exhaustion would soon overtake me, I spent a few minutes in prayer before starting to read - thanking God that our new extension was at last completed, and asking for His help in the days ahead as we all adjusted to our new family situation. I knew that I would be relying heavily on 'prayer power' and the sense of God's presence as I struggled to cope.

Opening the book, I began to read the first chapter, *Meditations among the Tombs*. Here James Hervey recorded thoughts which came to him while looking round an old village church in Cornwall. Admiring the handsome altar-piece, he pondered on the embellishment of places of worship as an expression of gratitude to God.

'Here I recollected and was charmed with Solomon's fine address to the Almighty, at the dedication of his famous temple ...   *But will God indeed dwell on earth? Behold! The heaven, and heaven of heavens, cannot contain thee; how much less this house that I have builded!*

Sleepily I smiled at the thought (however incongruous!) that, just like Solomon, I too had been addressing God after the completion of a building. Closing the book, I fell fast asleep.

The next day, still in need of spiritual reinforcement, I determined to go to the second Sunday morning service, at 11.15 at our local church. However, after I had taken Gran her breakfast and had a little chat with her, I suddenly felt that I was being told to hurry along to the *first* service, which began at 9.45am.

'But it's already a quarter to ten,' I objected silently. 'I'd have to walk in late, and I don't like that. It's embarrassing!'

'That doesn't matter. Just leave everything and go *now*,' I seemed to hear.

Somewhat intrigued, I obediently drove along to the church. For a couple of minutes I waited outside, while intimations were read out, concerning church activities in the coming week. Then, once the congregation had stood up to sing, I hurried in. Immediately after the hymn came the children's address.

The minister spoke of a guided tour he had recently given to local schoolchildren, showing them round the graveyard of the ruined church across the road - 'Alloway's auld haunted kirk', as Burns called it in his poem *Tam o' Shanter*. After pointing out the inscriptions on various old gravestones, including that of the poet's parents, he had told them about the determination and dedication of those who had built the 'new' church in which we were now sitting.

'Almost another case of *Meditations among the Tombs*', I thought with a smile.

A few minutes later, however, my amusement turned to amazement when he announced the Old Testament reading, from chapter 8 of the First Book of Kings: Solomon's prayer to God at the dedication of the new Temple! I sat transfixed as I heard again the words which I had read just before falling asleep the night before:

But can God indeed dwell upon earth? Heaven itself, the highest heaven, cannot contain thee; how much less this house which I have built! .... The passage continued: *Yet attend to the prayer and supplication of thy servant, O Lord my God, listen to the cry and the prayer which thy servant utters this day ....*

How comforted and fortified I felt by this startling coincidence! What had caused me to pick up that little book the night before, and open it at the appropriate place? - then insist that I go along *late* to the church and thus enter at precisely the 'right' part of the service? Once more I was awe-struck in my sudden awareness of this blessed invisible dimension, once more comparing it to a golden safety-net stretched out below a solitary tightrope-walker. I felt that the Holy Spirit had come to our aid again, bestowing a lovely, timely blessing on this new phase of our family life together, at the completion of the building of the extension to our home.

Chapter 8

Winged Comfort

The tea-maker alarm was beeping. Sleepily, I reached over to stop it. Nothing there. The persistent noise was coming from *behind* me. Why? Then I remembered. Yesterday Bob had been in pain again after his latest operation. More cancerous cells had been removed from his bladder and he was still passing blood. Groggy after the anaesthetic, he needed to sleep, but found it difficult to get into a comfortable position. That was why I had left our bed and come upstairs to the girls' room. Now that Sally was away at university, her bed was fortunately available for emergencies such as this. Hurriedly I sat up and reached across to stop the noisy alarm lest it waken Linda.

No, there was not a sound from the other bed, nor from Michael's bedroom across the landing. What day of the week was it? Saturday! Thank goodness. I poured out a cup of tea and sat up straight, cradling its warmth and marshalling my thoughts, ready to face the new day.

It was not yet seven o'clock. I still had a little precious time to myself. Soon Bob's mother would be up, slowly making her way to the kitchen to prepare her porridge, one of the few activities she could manage now that Parkinson's Disease had curtailed her former energy. Once she was back in her room I would give her the morning dose of medication and stop for a chat. In so doing, I would try to conceal my worries about Bob. How difficult it was to keep cheerful! But I knew that the slightest hint of anxiety would cause her to sink into a deep depression which would then have an adverse effect on Bob's fragile morale....

What else had I to do this morning? The usual jobs which had to be attended to on a Saturday: at least two loads of washing; tidying and cleaning the house. Linda and Michael would help - but would there be time to cook extra stew for the freezer? or to weed the garden? The ironing could wait until tomorrow evening, but I urgently needed to drive to the supermarket for next week's supplies. After that I would like to take the car to the car wash - but I'd better not stay away from home too long, just in case Bob might once again need to have emergency post-operative treatment at the hospital. And in any case I remembered that I had a pile of exam papers to correct. Somehow or other I would have to find a couple of hours before bedtime tomorrow to mark the French Listening Test so as to have the results ready for my colleagues on Monday morning.

'Dear God,' I prayed, 'please give me the strength I need to keep going. Help me to bear my heavy load cheerfully for my family's sake.'

All being well, I would manage to the church service the next morning. It seemed to me, not for the first time, that it was 'prayer power' alone that was keeping me going, like special 'petrol for my engine'. Every morning I prayed for strength to get through the day. On Sundays I always got an extra boost at the church service - often from the sermon, but often from something else too: the Bible reading, a prayer or hymn, a kindly smile from a friend, or simply the support I found in the togetherness of being with other believers....

Over the past difficult months I had set the alarm to go off early enough to allow time for meditation and relaxation. When completely relaxed, I would visualise myself in some beautiful tranquil place: on the sea shore or, often, in our own garden by moonlight. With such a comforting environment in mind, I would silently recite the Lord's Prayer, then pray to be shown the answer to any problem which was currently troubling me. In greater need than ever this Saturday morning, I made a determined effort to calm my overactive thoughts as, holding the still-warm cup, I prayed for strength.

But suddenly I found that I did not need to go through my usual routine of slowing down my breathing and gradually relaxing my body. With lightning speed I 'saw' myself - that is, my conscious self - leave my body and soar outside. Up, up I was rising, over the tall cypresses between our garden and our neighbours', swiftly down the nearby street to join the main road into the town, then gathering momentum down Ayr High Street to the harbour. A swift left turn and I was following the River Ayr to the sea. Soaring across the Firth of Clyde then over the mountainous island of Arran, I 'reached' the Kilbrannan Sound between the south end of Arran and the Mull of Kintyre. Ah, what an exhilarating sense of weightlessness and freedom!

All at once I was aware that I was no longer alone.

Three or four beings of light surrounded me. Using a silent means of communication, they imparted a message of comfort: that I was *never* alone or without support. They had come to remind me that my present difficulties were all part of the challenges which I had agreed to face so that my soul could progress. They were my friends and were supporting me. I was filled with a wonderful sense of love and belonging.

Then, their message delivered, they sped off again and I, too, swiftly returned by the way I had come, until my inner self was back in my body, and I found myself sitting up in bed, holding my cup of tea. That the cup was still upright, the tea not spilled, was a source of wonder to me. This powerful vision had not been a dream. If I had fallen asleep, even for a second, my fingers would have relaxed, letting the cup drop - as had happened on several previous occasions....

Incredulously I stared at the tea-maker clock. This amazing incident could have lasted only a minute or so - perhaps even less - but what a profound impression it had made on me. Like someone studying a beautiful piece of cut crystal, where each facet reflects a different colour of the spectrum, I pondered on all the various aspects of the vision: the out-of-the-body experience, the meeting-place, the angelic beings, the way in which they had addressed me. How wonderful to be assured that I was not alone and without support in my daily struggles to cope with all our difficulties. I felt that I had received a precious gift, which I could now treasure in the safe place of my memory, and which would henceforth bring me comfort and strength - as indeed it has over the past twenty years.

Chapter 9

Anniversary Message

It was on the day after our 18th wedding anniversary, that Bob and I had suffered the terrible shock of learning that he had cancer of the bladder. For the next four years, regular hospital treatment kept his illness in check, but eventually the specialist told him that he needed chemotherapy and radiotherapy. For this he spent six weeks in a Glasgow hospital, over thirty-five miles from our home. I visited him practically every day, but occasionally this was not possible, so we devised a little routine which would ensure continuity in the expression of our love for one another. Every night at eleven o'clock I would sit down at our dining room table, light a candle, and pray, asking God to bless Bob and our children and to grant us all courage and strength. At the same time, Bob would have the curtains pulled round his hospital bed, so that he could have privacy while he prayed for me and the children, and asked for God's blessing and help.

Alas, despite all the treatment, his physical condition

gradually worsened. (His spiritual strength increased, however.) He died just after 7am on the 26th of June - the day before our 23rd wedding anniversary.

It was a glorious sunny day, so when the minister came that afternoon to offer his condolences and to discuss the funeral arrangements, we sat outside in the back garden. I took out a small pile of books, in order to find ideas for possible readings and hymns: the Bible, the Church of Scotland hymn book, one or two volumes of poetry, and a paper back copy of William Barclay's *Prayers for Help and Healing*, which I had given to Bob when he was in hospital the year before. He had underlined the prayers which he had found most helpful.

About half-past three the minister said he had to go to another appointment. I decided that I would drive into town to register Bob's death. I would just make it to the registry office if I left immediately, so I gathered up the pile of books from the garden seat and hurried into the house to collect the necessary documents.

The next day had extra poignancy, bringing back, as it always did, memories of our happy wedding day, and I had to struggle to hold back the tears as I opened the curtains and gazed out over the sunny back garden.

The fresh appearance of the flowers and the damp earth showed that there must have been some light rain during the night. Suddenly, to my horror, I saw that one of the books was still on the garden seat - the precious book of prayers! Fearing that it had been spoiled by the rain, I rushed out to fetch it, wondering how I could possibly have been so careless. The front cover was indeed damp and had curled back - to reveal an inscription which (unknown to me) my beloved Bob had written there exactly one week before. My exasperation with myself turned into an indescribable mixture of grief and joy as I discovered these words, which seemed almost like an anniversary message:

> *20 June   Kath, my Madonna of the candle-light, I love you. Bob xxx*

Needless to say. every year at the end of June, the memory of that wonderful moment of discovery continues to bring me deep consolation in the midst of my sadness, and I thank God for this blessing.

Chapter 10

The Joyful Reunion

It was a dark, wet December afternoon, six months after Bob's death. The approaching New Year seemed the beginning of a dark empty future without him. As Sally and I waited at Preston railway station for the Manchester train, the bleak weather reflected my state of mind. In the Ladies' Room, which was drab and covered in graffiti, I thought in despair: 'Oh, I wish I could be somewhere else!' - *and suddenly I was!*

I 'saw' that I was now standing in a beautiful bathroom with aquamarine fittings. Beside the bath, which had a chrome grip in the middle of each side, there was a tall dark-green plant, with long pointed frond-like leaves reaching up to the ceiling. The plant-pot was a Victorian one: purplish-pink, with scalloped mother-o'-pearl edge, and resting on feet shaped like lion's paws. The window had plain, not obscure, glass and white net curtains. What impressed me most was the wonderful GOLDEN LIGHT streaming through the window and filling the whole room.

Full of wonder, I went over to the window and saw that I was on the first floor of a building - a hotel, I thought - overlooking a calm blue sea. Just below was the pavement, then the road, in an unusual light brown tar-macadam, a strip of grass, then the promenade and the sea. On my right the hotel wall followed the curve of the road, and the honey-coloured pebble-dash was bathed in the golden light. To my delight, I saw Bob standing on the pavement below. He looked well again, quite plump, wearing his favourite blue-grey sweatshirt and grey trousers. I knew he was waiting for me. I longed to run down and join him.

But suddenly I was once more in the dark depressing reality of Preston Station Ladies' Room. I had to fight back the tears as I returned to Sally.

Off we went to catch our train and sat down opposite each other with our magazines. But I just could not read, my eyes filling with tears as I thought with longing of Bob waiting for me in that beautiful place. Noticing my distress, Sally asked what was wrong. I began to tell her about my vision, but suddenly gasped as I realised that, like a film, it was continuing! I could see what was happening next, and could give Sally a running commentary! Two simultaneous realities!

I saw myself running down the dark-green carpeted stairs outside the bathroom to the double doors of the exit, which opened directly on to the street. Turning right, I ran along to Bob for a joyful reunion. We walked hand in hand across the road, along the prom and to the end of a little stone jetty. There we stood side by side, looking out to sea. We each took a coin, like a one-pound piece, and threw it down into the clear water, watching as the two coins sank to the bright dappled sand below. I knew that this was a symbolic payment we had to make. How I wished that we could stay together! - but knew that this was not possible, not *yet*, anyway. Then we walked back towards the road. On our left a little flight of stone steps led down to the water, where a rowing boat was waiting. It was varnished light brown, but with a white painted rim on which the oars rested. I realised that Bob would have to leave in it.

At the top of the steps we took a tender leave of one another. He said, 'Tell Sally that I love her too' - which immediately reinforced in me the feeling of simultaneous reality, the certainty that Bob was with me *at that moment*, though in a different place from Sally. Normally he would have sent his love not just to her but to all three of our children - but he knew that Sally was the only one with me just then. As he got into the boat and moved away, I understood that this was what he had to do - but knew also that he would come back again some day for me, and that consoled me.

And indeed, the memory of this vision has brought me comfort and strength ever since - especially the thought of that wonderful all-pervading golden LIGHT. I think of the words of the hymn:

> *In the heavenly country bright*
> *Need they no created light;*
> *Thou its light, its joy, its crown,*
> *Thou its sun which goes not down*

and I say a prayer of thanksgiving.

Chapter 11

O death, where is your sting?

Bayeux in Normandy was the holiday destination I had finally chosen for Michael and myself, after hours spent studying the map of France. It had been difficult to find a place that would suit both of us. For this was to be our first holiday together after Bob's death the previous year. As a modern languages teacher, I wanted to keep my French up-to-date, but my fifteen-year-old son was not particularly interested in trying to speak the language. However, as he was very keen on modern history, he agreed that it would be interesting to visit the Normandy beaches where the Allies landed on D-Day, the 6th of June, 1944.

Bayeux, the first town to be liberated, is, of course, also famous for the Bayeux Tapestry, created to commemorate the Norman Conquest of England in 1066. By coincidence, another (attempted) invasion of England - by the Spanish Armada in July 1588 - was being commemorated during the month of our visit, with a special issue of stamps by the British Post Office. These showed the powerful Spanish warships battling against heavy seas and the gale-force winds which blew them off course.

In Bayeux Michael and I visited the town's two main museums. One shows a replica of the wonderful tapestry, the other provides a detailed account of the 1944 Battle of Normandy. Both tell of invaders who crossed the English

Channel. Each mentions the problems of coping with the winds and tides. Each shows - one by pictorial tapestry, the other by contemporary newsreels - the cost, in terms of human lives, of such invasions.

We took a bus to Arromanches, to see one of the 1944 landing beaches. Beside a footpath leading down to the sand I noticed a rather decrepit memorial, erected after one of Napoleon's naval victories. Determined to conquer Europe, he had declared war on Great Britain... So many changes in the winds and tides of History itself! Former allies becoming enemies and then allies again. Why?

In nearly every Bayeux shop window there was a poster marking the 25th anniversary of the Treaty of Co-operation between France and West Germany. It showed the heads of the two leaders who had signed it: Charles de Gaulle and Konrad Adenauer. Yet this same Charles de Gaulle was to be seen every day on the war museum's black and white newsreel, striding along towards Bayeux with the Allied leaders, dead or surrendering German soldiers on each side of the road! The backdrop to these jubilant scenes of victory was Bayeux Cathedral with its distinctive twin spires, a cathedral built at the time of the Norman Conquest.

Just after leaving the war museum we crossed the road to visit the British War Cemetery. How beautifully kept it is! Immaculately trimmed lawns, red roses flowering amidst the hundreds of white gravestones. In one section of the cemetery, the pure white stones bear the names of young German soldiers killed in the same battle.

Deeply moved, I stood reading the loving inscriptions,

tender words from bereaved parents in memory of their sons. As my own young son moved slowly among the graves, I could see the twin spires of the cathedral in the distance, just as we had seen them only half an hour before in the old war news film, then the background to dreadful scenes of battle, but now to a place of great beauty and peace - peace bought at such a terrible price. I found it all so poignant that all I could do was sit down on a bench and just try to absorb the healing silence of that special place.

As I sat there, Michael came back to me. 'Mum,' he said, 'I've been reading the inscriptions and I came across a quotation I know, because I remember singing the words with the Youth Choir. Do you remember them?

O death, where is thy sting? O grave, where is thy victory?'

The very next morning, as I lay in bed - in the Hotel Churchill - I could hear voices coming from the dining room below. Happy German tourists, laughing and joking, were preparing to set off after their early breakfast. They were obviously enjoying their holiday in this place, which had, so comparatively recently, been enemy territory. Once again I found myself pondering, in some anguish, on the changes wrought by History, and on all the young lives - of all nations - lost in battle over the centuries. O God, *why?*

For comfort, I turned to the New Testament on my bedside table. It was a copy of the Gideons' International edition in three languages: French, German and English. I opened it - totally at random, as I thought - and the very first words my eyes fell on seemed to leap off the page at me. In awe and disbelief, and suddenly filled with a strange comforting warmth, I read the German version of the very same words that Michael had quoted to me the day before:

'Tod, wo ist dein Stachel? Hölle, wo ist dein Sieg?'

(Death, where is your sting? Grave, where is your victory?)

But, of course, on that page of the New Testament, the victory spoken of is Christ's triumphant victory *over death itself*. In my state of confusion and sadness, I was greatly comforted to be reminded once more that death is not the end, that the spirit survives, and that we live on. To all of us, God's children, whatever our nationality, whether victims of war or survivors of war, St. Paul's great words of reassurance ring out across the centuries:

Death has been swallowed up in victory. Death, where is your sting? Grave, where is your victory? ... Thanks be to God. He gives us the victory through our Lord Jesus Christ'.

Chapter 12

Pigeon

*'Across the tremendous bridge of sixteen hundred years
I come to stand in worship with you...'*

The powerful opening of Benjamin Britten's *St Nicholas* sprang into my mind as I gazed in astonishment at the page in front of me.

It was just after Easter. In need of spiritual renewal after a difficult winter beset with health worries, Bob and I had come on a little pilgrimage to the 'Holy Island' of Lindisfarne, off the coast of Northumberland. We were attracted by the prospect of seeing the facsimile of the famous Lindisfarne Gospels - and also by the novelty of driving across the three-mile causeway, which at low tide links the island to the mainland.

It had been cold and wet when we arrived in Berwick. Nevertheless we had decided to brave the elements and go straight on to Lindisfarne - that is, if the tide was right. I called in at the Berwick Tourist Office caravan to check and, reassured, was about to leave when my attention was caught by an unusual sight. Two young men had just entered. They were in overalls and had punk-style hair and earrings. One was gently carrying a young pigeon, which they had found on the ground nearby. The bird's head with its calm eyes and slightly curved bill remained perfectly still above the lad's interlaced fingers. And now, only a couple of hours later, how startled I was when my eyes fell on just such another bird's head above a similar interlacing of 'fingers' - but this time on a page of the thirteen-hundred year old Lindisfarne Gospels!

'Well, so what?' most people might say. But to me it was as if an electric current had suddenly made an arc across the centuries, opening my mind to the dedication and marvellous artistry of Eadfrith the scribe, who for at least two years had sat lovingly copying out the four Gospels in exquisite lettering, with wonderfully complex Celtic embellishments. As Bob and I sat, rain-soaked, in the Lindisfarne Hotel, gratefully warming our fingers round hot coffee cups, I thought how difficult it must have been in winter for Eadfrith to hold his pen steady enough to form the beautiful even letters and not to smudge his ink and forty-five different coloured pigments!

The striking immediacy of this visual coincidence remained with me - to such an extent that fifteen years later, when in London for a week's holiday, I resolved to seize the opportunity of viewing this book of Gospels in its original form at the new British Library.

First, however, I had to keep a promise to visit a former pupil and her young family in Kettering, Northamptonshire. Outside the local primary school, as we waited for the children, another mother was interested to learn that it had taken me just under an hour to fly from Prestwick to London Stansted airport. When I added that it took only seventy-five minutes from Prestwick to Beauvais in France, she exclaimed, 'Beauvais! That's where our racing pigeons were released from two weeks ago.'

The following day I stood in front of a glass case in the

British Library, gazing down at an open page of the original Lindisfarne Gospels. Tears of admiration, amazement and awe came into my eyes. Just why did I find this complex interweaving of strands so moving? I asked myself. Perhaps because there had been occasions when I, too, had used interwoven lines, not solely for the pleasure of creating a beautiful pattern - but in order to express an *idea*.

Over the past twenty years I had sometimes experienced such a remarkable *cluster* of coincidences that I had felt compelled to record them, not in my current diary, but in a separate album of their own, backing up my written account with relevant photographs. By underlining key words in different colours, I had been able to tease out each separate 'strand' from the memorable 'knot' of coincidences. For example, in my record of one such amazing cluster, I had, in that way, identified four specific recurrent themes: engraved stone archways; poets; the Saltire Society; and the preservation of old buildings. Finally I had decorated the front cover of the album with Celtic interlacing in the same four colours.

In this, my own humble way, I had been attempting to celebrate the wonderful network behind our everyday lives, made up of countless interconnected strands which bind together the seen and unseen, the network of which I had gradually become more aware over the years, sometimes dimly, sometimes acutely. How humble I felt now as I gazed down at the infinitely more complex interlacing of Eadfrith's amazing cross-carpet page.

Had the ancient Celts, his artistic predecessors, been

trying to express in visual terms *their* awareness of this unseen network when they invented such intricate patterns?

Beside the Gospels was an explanatory card stating that for Eadfrith this had been his '*opus dei*' - his major work, inspired by God. Food for thought. In the Underground on the way back to my daughter's home, I pondered on Eadfrith's wonderful achievement and, inspired, felt the resurgence of my own desire to produce - in however modest a way - my own '*opus dei*'. For several years I had had an increasing urge to share my treasured record of coincidences - even though I knew that this might possibly entail ridicule. Above all, I wanted to share the Good News that there is an ever-present unseen dimension beyond our visible material world, that death is not the end, that prayer is indeed answered, as Jesus promised: '*Ask, and you will receive; seek and you will find; knock, and the door will be opened.*'

As I approached Linda's flat, I resolved to set aside time each day for this project. I would certainly include an account of that memorable moment of 'recognition' on Lindisfarne when, catching sight of that bird-interlacing so soon after seeing the pigeon in the young man's hands, my eyes had suddenly been opened to 'see' in a different way.

The television news was just finishing as I entered Linda's living-room. In amazement I gazed at what was on the screen: a man holding a pigeon in his hands! The bird, released from Beauvais, had lost its way and had landed, exhausted, on the QE2! Once more the astonishing timing of an 'outside' event had coincided with, and confirmed my innermost thoughts...

Such coincidences are entirely beyond any 'normal' explanation. Only if we are prepared to take a leap into the unknown can we acknowledge them, accept them, and then pray for enlightenment as to *why* they have been given to us. In this particular case, I had received another powerful reminder of that timeless moment on Lindisfarne. Once again I recalled Britten's St Nicholas:

> *'Across the tremendous bridge of sixteen hundred years I come to stand in worship with you... Preserve the living faith for which your fathers fought, For faith was won by centuries of sacrifice And many martyrs died that you might worship God.'*

Chapter 13

Pedal Problems

'Frankly, Kathleen, I don't think you can manage this yet,' said my organ teacher. 'Not in time for the Music Festival at any rate.'

I had to agree. Despite several months of determined practice, the semi-quavers were just not flowing as they should! Bach had divided them equally among the three parts of this organ prelude. The two manual parts presented no problem but, after less than two years of organ tuition, my feet were as yet simply not expert enough in 'pedal geography' to keep up the required speed. How I wished I had started decades ago to learn the organ, instead of waiting until I retired! Humbly, I acknowledged that it had been I myself, not my teacher, who had proposed entering for the 'easier' of the two Festival organ classes. He knew very well it takes years of practice to acquire the necessary co-ordination of hands and feet. But it had amused me to think of entering for this Festival *fifty years* after I had first participated as a member of my school choir! Ah well, I would not now be able to indulge this whim...

But in no way was I discouraged from continuing to practise on this magnificent instrument, which I had loved for over half a century. How thrilled I had been by its resonant deep notes when the Junior Choir had been taken into the church to rehearse for the Christmas service!

Much more satisfying, I had decided (then aged nine), than the battered old piano in the church hall, where we went for our usual Friday practices and for Sunday School.

... The Sunday School! Suddenly I was reminded of a surprising incident, which occurred on my very first day there, just after my parents and I had moved to Ayr from Glasgow, our native city. An hour after our return from church we were having lunch when the telephone rang. My father answered it.

'Hello,' said a woman's voice. 'Is that Tom Hamilton, formerly of Dinmont Road, Glasgow? This is your old playmate, Gladys. My daughter Muriel told me that there was a new girl in her Sunday School class today - a Kathleen Hamilton. I thought I remembered hearing that you have a daughter of that name, so I got your phone number from the teacher. You must all come here for tea and a good chat.'

This was the beginning of a long friendship between Muriel and myself. Although she and her husband had travelled the world since their marriage, and her parents had moved to Jersey after their retirement, we had kept in touch. She and I had both been married in this church, our wedding music played on this splendid instrument. I remembered that, as Muriel walked down the aisle, the organist had played the Bach chorale *Sleepers Awake*!

... 'Bach chorale!' The words brought me back to the present, and to my disappointment concerning my pedalling. I resolved to take action. From now on I would begin each hour's organ practice with two of the progressive exercises in my book for beginners.

Two days later, as I drove home through the rain after an hour at the organ, I reflected on the results. I did feel a little more confident, but oh dear, how long it was going to take before I could achieve any fleetness of foot in my pedal-work? Ruefully, I thought of all the many hours of practice I had put into *Vater Unser im Himmelreich. (Our Father in Heaven)*. It was so frustrating - but my teacher was right: I just had to be patient. Coordination of my feet with my hands would take many, many hours of practice. As he often said: 'How do you eat an elephant? - Just one bite at a time!' Oh, I knew this was true, but I was still depressed as I arrived back home.

The postman had called in my absence with a pile of early Christmas cards. I recognised the handwriting on the topmost envelope. It was from Muriel! My jaw dropped in amazement as I read the message she had written opposite the usual Christmas greeting:

'You will be amused to hear that my 96-year-old very mixed-up Mamma said, à propos of nothing at all, to me on a recent visit: "My friend Kathleen Hamilton is learning to play the organ, but she can't reach the pedals, so she's having a lot of trouble.' Now since I've known about your organ-playing I'll never have mentioned it, since she has trouble understanding anything at all; so isn't that interesting!'

Interesting? It was absolutely astounding! Suffering as she did from senile dementia, and confined to an old people's home hundreds of miles away, how could Muriel's mother possibly have known about my organ playing? In particular, how could she have known about my *present* disappointment regarding pedalling? We had not seen one another for at least twenty-five years; I was therefore astonished that she even remembered my name. And, in any case, we had never known one another very well. Belonging to the rather formal generation of my parents, she would surely not have normally referred to me as "my friend Kathleen Hamilton" but rather as "my friend Tom Hamilton's daughter" or (to Muriel) "your friend Kathleen". What had prompted her to say these words? Above all, why had I received them just when I was preoccupied with my pedalling problem? There was absolutely no 'logical' explanation. It was, and must remain, a delicious enigma! Grinning with pleasure, I realised that I no longer minded about my slow progress in mastering the organ pedals. It had been worth it in order to receive and appreciate this glorious coincidental comfort.

**

The Music Festival organ class (advanced) took place on a windy March morning, in that same church. As a steward, sitting in the front pew next to the adjudicator, I had an excellent view of the only entrant's hands and feet as they moved effortlessly over the three manuals, the stops and the pedals. Full of admiration at the young man's skills, I thought of the many, many hours of hard work and determination which had produced this impressive performance. When the class was over and the young organist, the adjudicator and the small audience had left the building, I decided to stay on, in order to practise for my next lesson.

As a contrast to the howling wind outside, I chose a quiet, soothing piece, and had just reached the middle section when suddenly, over the sound of the gale, I heard a very loud prolonged cracking noise - followed by a terrifying crash. An enormous wooden cornice beam had fallen from the ceiling fifty feet above, landing on one of the pews just beside the central aisle! Anyone sitting there would have been killed instantly. Horrified, I ran to the office to fetch the church warden. As we approached the huge beam, I was appalled to see the six-inch rusty nails which protruded from it. What a tragedy would have occurred only twenty minutes earlier, if the beam had fallen on members of the audience! I felt faint at the very thought ...

For the rest of the day I was haunted by that dreadful long crack and the fearsome crash which had followed it. Still suffering from shock, I went to bed earlier than usual that evening, but lay there tossing and turning, unable to sleep. In need of comfort, I reached for my Bible and opened it at random, at Psalm 27. Immediately verses 4 and 5 seemed to spring off the page at me, and I was filled once more with awe and gratitude as I read:

One thing I ask of the Lord, one thing I seek:
That I may be constant in the house of the Lord
All the days of my life,
To gaze upon the beauty of the Lord
And to seek him in his temple.
For he will keep me safe beneath his roof
In the day of misfortune
He will hide me under the cover of his tent;
He will raise me beyond reach of distress.

'Thank you, thank you, Library Angel!' I murmured. 'And thank you, thank you, dear God, for keeping me safe.' With that, I relaxed into a deep sleep.

Chapter 14

Our Gospel armour

'South-west Scotland: this afternoon, cloud and rain will spread in from the Atlantic', said the radio announcer as I tipped the apples from the supermarket bag into a basin, ready for the Hallowe'en guisers I expected after dark; neighbours' children who would giggle as I tried to identify the child behind each mask, who would try 'dooking' for the apples bobbing in the water, then sing, recite a poem or tell some jokes in return for sweets and nuts. A pagan tradition, no doubt, but all harmless fun! Wasn't it ...?

Rain or no rain, my little dog was due his long Saturday afternoon walk. I decided to take him to Culzean Country Park about twenty miles away, so we set off in the car down the lovely coast road. As forecast, a grey mist had hidden the magnificent view. The Mull of Kintyre and the island of Arran had disappeared; only Holy Isle was still visible. I put on a cassette of Kenneth McKellar singing Handel arias, and sang along with him familiar items such as '*Comfort ye my people*' from *Messiah*. But as we were arriving at the Visitors' Centre car park, the beautiful aria was unfamiliar to me. From the cassette cover I found that it was '*Waft her, angels, to the skies*' from the oratorio *Jephtha*. Who was Jephtha? I wondered.

Looking up, I realised that the car park was empty. The castle and the Visitors' Centre had closed for the winter. However, the National Trust allows off-season visitors to walk in the extensive grounds, so I let Benji out, locked the car and turned round. And then I saw them!

Three adults on big horses, silent, motionless. Two men and a woman? It was hard to tell. The one in the middle was certainly smaller, with a hooded cloak, beneath which I caught a glimpse of a green-painted face. The other two wore masks over the green paint - one the most horrible I had ever seen: a death's head with fangs. All of the horses were bedecked with black plumes; two had docked tails, one interwoven with black crepe ribbon. There was no exchange of slightly embarrassed laughter at being seen in Hallowe'en costume, no banter, no talking at all. They seemed to be just silently waiting.

A strange uneasiness crept over me. My first reaction was to jump back into the car and drive Benji straight back into town. But he was already straining at the leash, desperate for his favourite walk along the cliff tops. I couldn't disappoint him.

As we made our way past the castle, above the sunken gardens, I was suddenly startled by a weird low sound from beyond the bare trees on the other side. Some kind of hunting-horn? No, probably just a stag bellowing in the deer-park, I told myself firmly. But as the deep baying sound came again, I caught sight of the three strange figures riding along the parallel road, in the same direction as myself. My blood ran cold. What if these sinister riders were suddenly to tower above me on the narrow cliff top path? Again I was strongly tempted to turn back.

Just then, however, a reassuringly ordinary figure appeared from the steps leading up from the gardens: a middle-aged lady with a spaniel at her heels. When I asked her if there was a special Hallowe'en event on that afternoon, she replied, 'No, everything has closed for the winter. I live here. There's nothing arranged for today. Perhaps they are from a local riding school?'

Thanking her, I walked on, still puzzled. Even supposing these were three perfectly ordinary friends dressed up for a bit of Hallowe'en fun, I couldn't help thinking that their minds and behaviour were bound to be affected by their hideous, frightening appearance and by their elevated position on horseback. Up there, they were bound to feel superior to 'lower' mortals, more powerful, deliberately terrifying. And why the black plumes and black tail-ribbon on the horses? I felt indignant that such beautiful innocent creatures should be involved in so ugly and sinister a ritual. For 'ritual' was the word that suddenly came into my head. I began to remember rumours of covens on the nearby hills.

My indignation grew into anger as we reached the narrow woodland path leading to the cliff top walk. 'Why should I turn back? I thought, as I kicked aside the dead leaves. 'After all, I'm a member of the National Trust, with as much right to be here as they have.'

True, but somehow this thought did nothing to allay the primitive fear which made me shudder at the thought of a possible confrontation on the deserted narrow path high above the jagged rocks. By now the grey mist was rolling in over the sea towards us. Holy Isle had completely disappeared.

'Holy Isle!' The name recalls the fact that a Christian hermit once lived there, a contemporary of Saint Columba. With profound gratitude I thought of the Christian missionaries who came across the sea to Scotland to spread the Good News, braving the cold and wet. Suddenly I grasped what a *difference* the coming of Christianity must have made to our forebears. On this, the old Celtic festival of Samhain, when people used to disguise themselves and light bonfires in order to chase away evil spirits, how easy it was to imagine their dread of the long winter darkness, their fear of the old pagan gods and malevolent ghosts, at a time when the Druids practised human sacrifice. On our way here, we passed a large standing-stone, not far from the cairn mentioned in Burns' *Tam o' Shanter*, 'where hunters fand the murder'd bairn' - believed to have been a site of pre-Christian rituals.

How wonderful to hear the Good News that each individual is precious to God the Father, that Jesus, His Son, sacrificed *Himself* for mankind, that we can invoke the Holy Ghost, the Comforter, far more powerful than any frightening earth-bound spirit. What protection the Christian converts must have found in the potent words of the Lord's Prayer: '... *deliver us from evil, for THINE is the kingdom, the POWER and the glory for ever, Amen.*'

I, too, found strength and courage in these same words as I marched along the cliff top path - Benji enjoying the quickened pace. Defiantly, I began to sing John Bunyan's famous hymn, '*Who would true valour see*', savouring especially: '*Hobgoblin nor foul fiend shall daunt his spirit!*' then all the verses of '*Soldiers of Christ arise, and put your armour on*' as I stamped along. For added protection, I visualised the poster in my kitchen: a knight riding off into battle, above St Paul's powerful words to the Ephesians (Chapter 6): *Therefore, take up God's armour ... Stand firm, I say. Fasten on the belt of truth, for coat of mail put on integrity; let the shoes on your feet be the gospel of peace, to give you firm footing; and with all these take up the great shield of faith, with which you will be able to quench all the flaming arrows of the evil one. Take salvation for helmet; for sword take that which the Spirit gives you - the words that come from God*'.

In church the next morning, All Saints' Day, there occurred a startling coincidence, one of the kind I have come to call a 'confirmatory coincidence'. After the children (including some of my little guisers of the night before) had trooped off to Sunday School, the minister read the Old Testament lesson, from Chapter 11 of the Book of Judges. The hairs on the back of my neck stood on end as I learned the answer to my previous day's question: Who was Jephtha? - He was the king who, as the result of a thoughtless vow, had to offer up his beloved only daughter as a human sacrifice.

Who the strange riders were I still don't know - but this I *do* know: Thanks be to God for the Good News, and for our 'gospel armour!'

Chapter 15

An Invisible Angel?

'Quick, God, please! Help me! I don't know what to do next!' I prayed desperately as the woman in the passenger seat reached once again for my throat. My hand tightened on the steering wheel and, with tears obscuring my vision, I struggled to keep the car on a straight course.

My distress was caused not by my friend Sheila's hand on my throat, but my inability to reply to her kind invitation. Profoundly deaf and with severely impaired eyesight, Sheila has learned to read responses by lightly placing her fingertips on her friends' throats and peering hard at their lips, a trick taught her at an early age by her mother, who was anxious to integrate her third daughter into family life without recourse to sign language. The latter Sheila learned at school, but as I have never learned to sign, we use the 'throat method' when we are together.

The two of us were travelling to my favourite Country Park, Culzean, in order to walk my dog. Sheila had just asked if I would accompany her the next morning to the church near my former home, followed by lunch at the nearby tourist centre, where she wanted to buy some gifts before returning home to Middlesex. The friends whom she usually visited on a Sunday in Scotland were on holiday, and so she would be alone for the whole day. Now she was waiting for my answer.

My heart sank. Not only was I on door duty at my new

church the following morning, but it would be my elderly mother's birthday. She had dementia and I knew that she would be further confused by the sight of Sheila clutching at my throat! Conversation would be well-nigh impossible - and in any case I knew from experience that I would need all my energy just to cope with my mother. On the other hand, I hated the idea of Sheila spending a lonely Sunday so far from home - especially in the light of what she had just told me ...

How smart she had looked when I arrived at her hotel that morning. Bright cheerful clothes in navy and red, hair glamourously styled. Has she got a new man friend? I wondered, remembering our last meeting two years before. Then, after telling me sadly about her husband Lindsay's sudden death, she had asked me if I, also a widow, ever thought of marrying again.

'It's so lonely without him. I'd love to have the company of another husband,' she had said wistfully.

Now, in the car, she was up-dating me on what had happened in her life since then. Horrified, I heard of her discovery of a lump in her breast, the mastectomy, chemotherapy and subsequent hair loss. So her smart coiffure was, in fact, a wig. Profound sympathy mixed with admiration for her courage brought the tears to my eyes as she added a further sad piece of news.

Lindsay's mother had died earlier that week. Usually Sheila would visit her mother-in-law in Newcastle on her return south after a weekend in Ayr. This time, however, she had gone to Newcastle first, to attend the funeral, before taking the train to Ayr. On Monday she would travel straight back to Middlesex, ready to start her part-time work - an administrative post with SENSE, the charity for the deaf-blind.

'Oh please, dear God, help me to help Sheila,' I begged silently as, arriving at the Country Park, we drove downhill towards the Visitors' Centre car park.

A cup of tea was our first priority. Because dogs are not allowed inside the tearoom, we made for the unoccupied table outside and sat down beside one another on a wooden bench, so that Sheila could continue to feel the vibrations in my throat during our conversation.

Suddenly I caught sight of three ladies looking for spare seats at a table. As I indicated to them that the bench opposite was free, I saw that one was my friend Rena, accompanied by her former neighbour. Rena introduced us. The third lady was the neighbour's daughter - who instantly realised why Sheila was touching my throat. To my delight, she immediately began to communicate with my friend in sign language! As she did so, she relayed their conversation to the rest of us. How amazed we were to learn the following:

she too was called Sheila
she too worked for SENSE
she too had come to Ayr for the weekend
she too had travelled to Ayr from Newcastle (where she lived)
she too was meaning to attend my former church the next morning
she too wanted to have lunch at the Tourist centre (with her mother)
she too intended to buy souvenirs there afterwards

Hearing of my dilemma, she immediately offered to collect Sheila the next morning and take her to church, followed by lunch at the Tourist Centre!

Astounded by this swift answer to my prayer, I laughed aloud in delighted gratitude. It was almost as if I could reach out and touch an invisible angel who had come to our aid. 'I can just about hear the rustle of wings!' I exclaimed jokingly, and, turning to look over my shoulder, added, 'Thank you, angel, wherever you are!'

We all marvelled at this astonishing series of coincidences, and lifted our teacups in a common act of thanksgiving.

Chapter 16

September 11

Have coincidences any relevance to the way we look at life? Can they offer reassurance that there is something better beyond all the violence, ugliness and evil, about which we constantly hear on our daily news?

I am no politician, just an ordinary member of the public, often deeply troubled about my inability to change things for good. Nor am I a philosopher, claiming to be able to explain the mysterious ways in which coincidences occur. Having personally experienced anguish, loss and desolation, I shudder and weep in horror, as millions of others do, when confronted by images of terrible suffering: the abduction and murder of little children, ethnic cleansing, the bombing of innocent civilians. Over the years, reports of natural disasters- earthquakes, typhoons, floods, famine - have also appalled me, and made me question my belief in a God who created 'all things bright and beautiful'. Looking back over the last half-century, I can remember many such times of horror.

But ...

But I can also recall many, many moments of profound happiness, of astonished joy, and above all, of awe and wonder, as I have gradually become aware of the unseen dimension beyond the outward appearances of this life. Despite all the doom and gloom of the news bulletins, I just cannot ignore and forget all the occasions when my urgent prayers for help were answered, and when at times of spiritual darkness, amazing coincidences suddenly lit up the way ahead. At such moments I have found it absolutely impossible to doubt the existence of God.

Tuesday 11 September 2001. That morning my alarm went off earlier than usual. I had set it to ring at seven o'clock so that I could have the luxury of reading my new book for half an hour, before getting up to make breakfast. My friend Marie had arrived from France the previous afternoon, and I had promised to take her on a day excursion to the island of Arran. We had arranged to have breakfast at eight o'clock, so that we could set off in good time to catch the morning ferry.

The new book, a present from Marie, was a visual delight. It presented a series of paintings of the Annunciation by the Italian Renaissance artist Fra Angelico. Each painting was shown in full and in sections, with fascinating explanations of the symbolic detail in the background, as the Archangel Gabriel announced to the Virgin Mary that she was to bear a son who would be called Jesus. I reflected that Gabriel - 'messenger of God' - appears not only in Christian but also in Jewish and Moslem tradition. It is he who, in the Old Testament, interprets Daniel's vision, and it is likewise Gabriel who is said to have revealed the sacred writing of the Koran to the prophet Mohammed.

Smiling with pleasure at the loving precision with which the artist had painted each feather of Gabriel's wings, I noted that their magnificent hues were colour co-ordinated to match his robes. Such detail! - quite unlike the vague shape of the *Entité Ailée* (Winged Being) which I had discovered recently in London's Tate Modern gallery. There the smooth, simple white outline of that alabaster sculpture had immediately reminded me of the bright, but indistinct, beings who had comforted me, in my vision of our meeting high above the Kilbrannan Sound. Had the sculptor been trying to convey a similar vision of a 'being of light' - apparently winged, but without visible feathers? Marie and I would see the Kilbrannan Sound later in the day, from the far side of Arran. I would refrain from mentioning my angelic comforters, though, lest my friend think me very odd ...

But when I went downstairs to prepare the breakfast, I soon realised that the trip to Arran would not, after all, take place. Marie, waiting for me in the living room, was pale, and complained of an acute pain in her stomach. Instead of rushing off to catch the morning ferry, we had to arrange for an emergency appointment at the local surgery. However, the doctor could find no explanation for the pain. By early afternoon it had disappeared as mysteriously as it had come, so we decided to make the most of the sunshine by visiting Culzean Country Park, which I always like to show to my guests.

The distant blue mountains, the sparkling expanse of sea below the cliff tops where we strolled, looking out for seals and gannets, then the warmth of the sunlit garden, as we sat beside the bright herbaceous borders, listening to the splash of the fountain - such are my memories of those two precious hours of tranquillity, before we were suddenly made aware of the sinister shadow of terrorism which that day had been cast across the world.

Driving out of the car park, I switched on the car radio for some music. Instead, a news bulletin was being broadcast: the horrific report of the terrorist attack on the World Trade Center in New York. Appalled, we fell silent as we heard the dreadful details, instinctively yearning to be able to do something to ease the terrible suffering of our fellow human beings. How impossibly useless I felt ... All I could do was put up an urgent silent prayer: 'Oh please, God, please send angels quickly - to receive the dead, to support the dying, to be present with the bereaved, to strengthen all those who are desperately afraid that they have lost a loved one. Oh please, God, send a host of angels, and please send them *now*! Only a whole host of angels can help in this terrible situation. Oh please, God, quickly, send Your angels to help!'

Back at home we - like millions of others - gazed in horror at the television images. Again and again we were shown the two planes crashing, one after the other, into the twin towers, the terrifying flames, the slow, inevitable collapse of each building, the unspeakably horrific sight of victims jumping out of the windows to certain death below, pedestrians fleeing in order to escape the huge clouds of white dust surging down the streets after them. Finally, unable to bear it any longer, we turned off the television set and attempted to have a rational discussion about the possible motives for the attack. In vain! The traumatic scenes we had witnessed were still far too vivid in our minds. As we tried desperately to come to terms with this latest sinister turn in world affairs, we slowly began to realise how great was the threat posed by international terrorism. Emotionally drained, we eventually gave up trying to find adequate words, and

Marie retired to her bedroom, while I pottered around in the kitchen, trying to calm my racing thoughts.

When, finally on my way to bed, I was about to switch off the lamp on the upstairs landing, my attention was suddenly drawn to a book on the bookshelf immediately below it. Before I had even seen what the title was, I felt strongly prompted to pull it out and open it. *Millennium Eyewitness* on the front cover reminded me that this was a book which I had bought at the beginning of the previous year, 2000, but into which I had only occasionally dipped. It was a collection of short eyewitness accounts of notable events over the past thousand years. Opening it totally at random, I found myself gazing at a page which I had not read before: the description of a tragic incident on London in 1623. Once again I felt as if I were standing in a mysterious timeless ellipse as, rooted to the spot, I read the following:

THE COLLAPSE OF A CHURCH AT BLACKFRIARS, ENGLAND (Thomas Goad)

(...) Such was the noise of this dreadful and unexpected downfall that the whole city of London presently rang of it, and forthwith the officers of the city (to whom the care of good order chiefly appertaineth) and in special Sergeant Finch, the Recorder, repaired thither the same evening. (...) With all speed possible some were employed for the relieving and saving such as yet struggled for life under this heavy load; which could not so soon be effected as they in charity desired, for that the ruins, which oppressed the sufferers, did also stop up the entrance to the helpers, who were fain to make a breach in through an upper

window of stone. From whence they hasted down with pickaxes and other instruments, to force asunder and take off by piecemeal the oppressing load of beams, joists and boards. At the opening thereof, what a chaos! What fearful objects! What lamentable representations! Here some bruised, some dismembered, some only parts of men; there some wounded and weltering in their own and others' blood, other some putting forth their fainting hands and crying out for help. Here some gasping and panting for breath, others stifled for want of breath. To the most of them being thus covered with dust, this their death was a kind of burial ...

What was I to make of this appallingly appropriate coincidence, to which I felt quite sure that I had been directed? It was hardly a consolation to know that, over 300 years ago, other people had suffered the same awful death when a building collapsed. I noticed from the introductory notes that Thomas Goad was a rector, who wrote theological tracts. No doubt he and his contemporaries had struggled to come to terms with that horrific event, just as we were now trying so desperately to do with this day's terrible tragedy. Then, as now, the anguished cry must have gone up: 'Oh God, why did You let this happen? Where were You today?' Or, indeed, the bitter question: 'How can anyone claim that there this a loving God, when something so ghastly as this can happen?'

Pondering on what consolation - if any - a minister of the Gospel could possibly offer his flock in such dreadful circumstances, I was suddenly reminded of Luke's account of Jesus' anguish on the Mount of Olives, just before the betrayal which led to his crucifixion:

Then he went out and made his way as usual to the Mount of Olives, accompanied by his disciples. When he reached the place he said to them, 'Pray that you may be spared the hour of testing'. He himself withdrew from them about a stone's throw, knelt down, and began to pray: 'Father, if it be thy will, take this cup away from me. Yet not my will but thine be done.' And now there appeared to him an angel from heaven bringing him strength, and in anguish of spirit he prayed more urgently; and his sweat was like clots of blood falling to the ground. When he rose from prayer and came to the disciples he found them asleep, worn out by grief. 'Why are you sleeping?' he said. Rise and pray that you may be spared the test.'
(Luke 22, verses 39-46).

'An angel from heaven bringing him strength' ... Remembering my instant, instinctive reaction on first hearing of the terrorist attack - a desperate prayer for angels to strengthen and support all the victims - I was startled by another coincidence. For years after this day's traumatic events, people would no doubt say, 'I remember exactly where I was when I first heard the shocking news' - just as older folk still did nearly forty years after President Kennedy's assassination. And where had I been today when I heard that dreadful radio report?

I had been at the exact spot at Culzean where, a few years before, I had shuddered at the sight of the sinister Hallowe'en riders, silently waiting there, high up on their black-plumed horses.

But ...

But that was also only about two hundred yards from the very place where my urgent prayer for help for my deaf friend Sheila had been so swiftly answered, with such an amazing series of coincidences that I had spontaneously called out 'Thank you!' - joking that I could almost hear the rustle of an angel's wings! With renewed intensity, I prayed once more for all the victims and their families, and for all the fire-fighters and police trying so desperately to rescue those still trapped under the rubble.

• • •

Footnote. Ten days later, on 21 September, there appeared a heart-rending photograph of the first baby born to a widow of the terrorist attack. I have kept this deeply moving picture of the young mother kissing her tiny son - the son she named Gabriel.

Chapter 17

Loneliness

How lonely one can feel in a crowd! Sitting in a packed theatre, looking in vain for just one familiar face, I reflected sadly that I now felt a complete stranger in Glasgow, the city where I had spent the first happy eight years of my life, and where I had later been a student for five years. Fondly, I recalled the Christmas and New Year parties in our large extended family; my special friends at primary school; the close fellowship I had enjoyed with my fellow students at university and teacher training college.

Now all that belonged in the past. My grandparents, my father and most of my aunts and uncles were dead, cousins and friends dispersed throughout the world.

'So do things pass away, like a tale that is told,' I quoted sorrowfully to myself, as other members of the audience went off in little groups during the interval for a convivial drink at the bar.

Suddenly, however, I thought of my college friend, Margaret. *She* was still living locally, on the outskirts of the city, as I knew from the Christmas cards she had sent over the years. Like me, she was now married with a family, and no doubt very busy, but surely we could find time to meet for a chat somewhere in the city centre? This thought cheered me up, and I resolved to contact her. *At that very moment* I became aware of a person who had just arrived on my left-hand side and who was now standing all alone, leaning against a pillar. It was none other than Margaret! In order to re-establish contact, all I had to do was reach out and touch her.

• • •

This little incident, however apparently insignificant to an outside observer, had, over the years, become one of my most treasured memories. Not only because the amazingly coincidental meeting brought me comfort just when I needed it, but also because it was a striking example of a phenomenon which I had then already begun to notice: namely, a totally unexpected *external* event which corresponds exactly with an *inner* preoccupation, often bringing a solution to a problem.

Fifteen years after that reunion at the theatre, I found myself in another situation where I was facing loneliness - but this time on a much greater scale. After over twenty-five precious years of busy, fulfilling family life, I was having to come to terms with the 'empty nest syndrome'. Bob and his mother had both died; Sally, happily married, was settled in Belfast; Linda had a good job in London; Michael was enjoying student life in Aberdeen with a circle of new friends. Lonely and bereft of my former role, that of home-maker for husband and children, I prayed for guidance and for a new sense of identity.

Before the beginning of the school autumn term, I felt prompted to spend a couple of nights in Galloway, in the south-west corner of Scotland. Knowing nobody at all in the whole region, I was delighted when Michael offered to come with me. As destinations I chose two places which I knew and liked, but which my son had never visited:

Whithorn and Portpatrick. With Benji on the back seat, we set off in my car, relishing the quietness of the roads, the austere beauty of the Southern Uplands, then the lush farmland as we approached the Solway Firth. Whithorn and Portpatrick are both in Wigtownshire, but on two separate promontories, on either side of Luce Bay. From Whithorn, on the south-east of the one known as The Machars, there are views over to the mountains of the English Lake District, whilst Portpatrick, on the west side of the Rhins of Galloway, faces towards Ireland.

The next morning, over breakfast in the picturesque little town of Kirkcudbright, we made our plans for the day. Whithorn would be our first 'place of pilgrimage', as I called it - only half jokingly, because for many centuries the kings and queens of Scotland had indeed made pilgrimages to this, the place where St Ninian had founded the very first Christian community in Scotland. That was in the 5th century AD, a hundred years before St Columba arrived on Iona. Remembering the comfort and inspiration I had gained from the little pilgrimages which Bob and I had made to Iona and Lindisfarne, I was aware that another reason for my choosing Whithorn - a place still regarded by many as holy - was my present need of spiritual renewal. But in addition there was currently something else in that little town which I hoped would be of interest to Michael: an archeological dig. We agreed that if we set off early enough, we could see Whithorn before lunch, then drive across to Portpatrick. There we could spend an energetic afternoon walking Benji along the magnificent cliff-top paths. However, *'Man proposes, God disposes!'*

Our departure was delayed when I discovered that my wristwatch needed a new battery. Because we took a while to find a shop with one of the correct size, it was nearly noon when we drove down Whithorn's broad main street. Approaching the tourist centre, I suddenly remembered that this place had cropped up in conversation the previous autumn, at a family wedding. My mother's widowed cousin, a retired head teacher, whom I had met only two or three times in my life, had told me that she had a part-time job here. So, it was not quite true that I knew nobody in the whole of Galloway! However, Betty had mentioned that she did not live in Whithorn but in a little village several miles away, the name of which I had forgotten. And when I enquired at the reception desk, the girl shook her head.

'No, sorry. Mrs Mackintosh isn't often here nowadays. She's trying to sell her house.'

She began to give me rather complicated directions to Betty's school house, but I stopped her, saying that once we had been on the guided tour of the historic site, we would prefer to take the recommended walk to St Ninian's Cave. Our dog needed the exercise - and so did we!

As the next guided tour was not due to start for another twenty-five minutes, we made our way to a café, where, because of Benji, we sat outside, at a table on the pavement. While we were waiting for our drinks, a lady hurried past into the butcher's shop next door. She looked rather familiar. Could this by any remote chance be Betty Mackintosh? Having met her so seldom, I had difficulty in recalling her exact features. This lady was casually dressed, in trousers, quite unlike the wedding finery Betty had been wearing last September.

When she reappeared, and was about to hurry past, I tapped her on the arm, saying, 'Excuse me, is it Mrs Mackintosh?'

'Yes!' she replied, stopping to look at us quizzically. Exclamations of surprise and delight followed, on both sides! She then invited us to come to her home for tea after our afternoon walk.

'Excuse me if I dash off now,' she said apologetically. 'It's half-day closing here today. I'm just rushing round the shops before they shut.'

So, our paths had crossed in the two brief minutes she had taken to hurry in and out of the butcher's shop, where we just 'happened' to be at that precise time! When I thought of how Michael and I had originally intended to 'do' Whithorn much earlier that morning, the irritation I had felt at the delay melted away, as I marvelled at the wondrous way in which we had been brought together. To make contact with the only person I knew in the whole of Galloway, I had only to reach out and touch her!

Needless to say, this reminded me of my remarkable reunion with Margaret, and later, as we sipped tea in Betty's lovely garden, I told her and Michael about that surprising incident in the theatre fifteen years before.

The next day was rather dull, with rain threatening, but I was determined to show Michael Portpatrick, so we set off for the Rhins of Galloway. From Portpatrick's quaint little harbour we had the choice of two cliff-top walks. To the south the path leading to the ruins of Dunskey Castle was, I remembered, remarkable for its rich variety of wild flowers. However Michael, looking at the map, pointed out that the one to the north was preferable, as it eventually dropped down to Sandeel Bay, where Benji could be safely let off the lead for a good run.

By now, mist and fine rain had obscured the horizon and most of the sea, but once we had climbed up the steep steps from the harbour we had a splendid view of seabirds' nests on the rocky ledges far below, and so we pressed on cheerfully despite the drizzle. I peered through the mist, trying to glimpse the nearby lighthouse - but in vain! The few people we encountered were all wisely heading in the opposite direction, seeking shelter in the village. When heavier rain began to fall, we too began to think of turning back, but just then we caught sight of the deserted little bay where Benji could have his promised run.

We began to descend the steep path, Michael and Benji leading the way. Halfway down we were surprised to see a solitary figure in front of us, that of a woman, who stepped aside on to a tiny grassy ledge above a rocky inlet. There she bent down to pick some wild flowers. Catching sight of her face, Michael stopped short in disbelief, then turned back towards me with a startled look.

'I think it's your friend Margaret!' he mouthed silently.

'Margaret? I called tentatively.

'Goodness, Kathleen, whatever are *you* doing here?' she exclaimed.

It was indeed my college friend! Less than twenty-four

hours after I had told the story of our surprise meeting at the theatre, she had made another totally unexpected appearance in a place where I had thought I knew nobody.

Back at home, I made the following entry in my diary:

'Michael and I were away for only fifty-four hours or so, but in that time we had two such amazingly coincidental meetings that I felt we were indeed being led.

'Here I pause, hesitating to say 'led by *God*', because I feel too humble and unimportant to have God Himself leading me! 'Unseen helper' - yes, I could allow myself to write that; 'my guardian angel' - perhaps! But '*God*'? And yet it is to God that I pray for help and guidance. Definitely to God. Not 'Please lead me, unseen helper'. Not 'Dear guardian angel, please help me', but 'Oh God, dear Heavenly Father, please lead me, please restore my soul'. And - thank God! - prayers like that are answered. It may be that God delegates His angels to help, or even that departed souls are sometimes permitted to return to help loved ones in need. Who knows? How could I ever claim to know the answer? To quote the motto of one of my favourite French writers, Montaigne: '*Que sçais-je?*' (What do I know?) At this earthly level, I can't know, can only guess, can only hold up my hands in blind faith and ask for help. It would be futile - and presumptuous - to try to offer a rational solution to this profound mystery.

'But Jesus understood how the system works - of that I am sure! And so, in my puzzlement, I find it helpful and comforting to re-read His words as quoted by John (chapter 14, verses 14-17):

If you ask anything in my name, I will do it. If you love me you will obey my commands; and I will ask the Father, and he will give you another to be your Advocate, who will be with you for ever - the Spirit of truth. The world cannot receive him, because the world neither sees nor knows him; but you know him, because he dwells with you and is in you.

In other words, the Holy Spirit, to which we have access through prayer. I am beginning to appreciate more and more the concept of the trinity, i.e. God the Father, God the Son, and God the Holy Spirit.

'Now, before I go to bed, I just want to finish by recording here my profound gratitude for this most recent evidence of an invisible source of help, for the renewal of my deeply-held belief that we are never totally alone, but are led by God, as sheep are led by a shepherd.'

Before that start of the autumn term, I made a poster for my kitchen, carefully copying out a quotation from chapter 16 of John's Gospel: words spoken by Jesus on that loneliest of nights - the one when He was betrayed by one of His own disciples, and when He knew that He was about to be put to death.
Yet I am not alone, because the Father is with me.
I have told you all this so that in me you may find peace.
In the world you will have trouble. But courage!
The victory is mine;
I have conquered the world.

Chapter 18

Like a Shepherd

'Kath, would you like to sing the first part of this duet with me at the Christmas concert?' asked Marion, my former next-door neighbour. After five years of living alone, I had moved to a smaller house, but Marion and I had remained good friends.

I felt very honoured to be asked, but also somewhat apprehensive. Marion loves singing, and I used to enjoy listening to her pure, melodious soprano voice as she practised in her kitchen for her next lesson. Although I, too, love to sing, my voice is untrained, and because I have never mastered proper breath control, I always fear that I shall run out of air before the end of a phrase. But Marion has kindly encouraged me to sing duets with her at concerts, and I find great pleasure in the contralto parts, trying my best to harmonise exactly with her high notes.

What she had in mind this time, however, was quite different from our usual two-part songs. It could not really be called a 'duet'. In this double aria from Handel's *Messiah*, the contralto sings the first part all alone, followed by the soaring soprano solo, in a higher key. The thought of performing the contralto solo in public filled me with alarm! 'Just concentrate on getting the message across to the audience', coaxed Marion.

The message. What exactly *is* the message of this aria? I thought it over. It reinforces the oratorio's wonderful opening: *Comfort ye, comfort ye my people.* First there is the prophetic description of the Messiah (the Saviour): *He shall feed his flock like a shepherd,* then the invitation: *Come unto him, all ye that labour ... and he will give you rest.* Yes, the solace and reassurance contained in these words were certainly worth conveying to our listeners ... Plucking up all my courage, I told Marion that I would practise my breathing exercises and try my best.

'Like a shepherd' ... I pondered on the many occasions when I have thought of God in this way: as a shepherd leading his flock to pasture. Judging by how often crematorium hymnbooks fall open at Psalm 23, *The Lord's my Shepherd*, this is an image beloved of many, many other people too, when they are in mourning after the death of a loved one. But it is not only at times of bereavement that I have come to be aware of God's reassuring presence. Over the past thirty years, since I began keeping my private diaries, I have come to trust the Good Shepherd *every day*, to provide me with both physical and spiritual food, and to lead me along life's path - whether that be through tangled thorns, over steep rocks or 'beside the still waters'.

Re-reading these many notebooks, in which I have recorded not only sorrows but also personal joys, I am struck by how often I have written *'Deo gratias'* ('Thanks be to God') at the end of an entry. So many blessings, too numerous to retain in my conscious memory. How glad I am that I noted them as they occurred - especially the coincidences, which big or small, have gladdened my heart on my journey, some giving me new strength when my legs were weary, others just lightening my step by making me laugh.

However, the most memorable coincidences have been those which, at dark and difficult times, have served to show me the way ahead when, in my blind confusion and distress, I have relied *entirely* on God for guidance.

In particular, I remember one such occasion when the recurring theme of *shepherd and sheep* reinforced in me the comforting conviction that God, the Good Shepherd, was indeed leading me, providing me with much-needed rest and spiritual nourishment. I recorded it during two luminous autumn days on the island of Arran - a blessed little time of respite in a period of great anguish.

Only months after the death of my mother-in-law, it was becoming painfully evident that my beloved Bob's cancer had now reached the terminal stage. With the future so uncertain, we forced ourselves to think only of the present, living one day at a time - sometimes, in the midst of yet another emergency, only one *minute* at a time. Struggling meanwhile to cope with my demanding teaching job, I depended completely on 'prayer-power' to give me enough strength to support the two of us and our three children, physically, emotionally and spiritually. That October, in a brief period of remission, Bob had urged me to take advantage of the unusually fine weather and go off on my own for a couple of days' rest.

It was then that I made the following notes in my diary, and it is with these that I wish to conclude my testimony, *Joyful Witness*.

'Brodick, Arran, 16 October.

'Yesterday morning the ferry from Ardrossan was delayed for half an hour while it was being refuelled. But I did not mind at all; I just revelled in being on board. Had my camera not been at the foot of my overnight bag, I would have taken photographs of two large floats loaded with hay for the Arran *animals* beside a very large supermarket container full of food for the Arran *people*.

'This morning, after a good night's sleep, I walked from Brodick to Lamlash. I hope that my photographs turn out well, to remind me of all the loveliness I found on that road to gladden my heart. Photo-graph: writing with *light!* What a precious record this makes, often more eloquent than mere words. These are some of the things I remember especially:

– Coming up behind an old lady who was slowly climbing up the steep hill out of Brodick.

'It's a stey brae', she said, and was pleased when I replied, 'Yes, as they say: "Set a stout heart to a stey brae"' (a steep hill).

– The new cemetery with its six gravestones and two marker posts. Several had fresh flowers in front of them. After reading the inscriptions, I climbed a little farther up the grassy slope and turned to look back, glad to feel the warmth of the sun behind me. Noticing that my shadow was pointing towards the distant peak of Goatfell, I felt a sudden urge to take a photograph. As I peered through the view-finder, I positioned myself so that my shadow would be in direct alignment with the mountain-top. The new graves would be in the foreground of the picture; my moving shadow seemed to emphasise that I was the only person still alive in this little place. Suddenly, just as I clicked the shutter, a wonderful coincidence occurred. Two things happened simultaneously: I felt impressed upon me the words: *'While you still have a shadow, feed my sheep'*, and then, *at that very moment*, a large float piled high with hay (i.e. animal feed) went past. I hope it is in the photograph, to remind me of this perfectly-timed reinforcement of the words which I 'heard'.

– Gladness to be striding along strongly, with my feet on God's earth, not enclosed in a car, which would have meant missing all the quietness and birdsong, and not even on a bicycle, which would have gone too fast and been an encumbrance on the steep hills.

– The lovely, *blessed* warmth and brightness of the sunny day - amazing for this time of year.

– Gorgeous red dahlias in the Lamlash gardens, also cheerful yellow winter jasmine, already in full flower.

'I wandered along the sheltered seafront, enjoying the view across to Holy Isle, where an Irish visionary, a contemporary of St Columba, lived for many years. Halfway along the village street there is a raised circular bed with three enormous stones, bigger than the ancient standing stones which I had just passed on the road. They were set up here at the request of a group of descendants of Arran folk, who now live in Canada and North America, but who came over here in 1977 on a pilgrimage, to commemorate their forebears, victims of the Highland Clearances.

On one of the stones there is an inscription, stating that at this place some 87 souls gathered before setting off across the Atlantic on 25 April 1829. Standing on the Mound opposite, the Rev. Mackay preached to them, basing his sermon on 1 Peter 5, verse 7: *Casting all your care upon him, for he careth for you.*

Later, when I looked this up in my New English Bible, I found three other verses of the same chapter which I like, chiefly because they are another reminder of the words I received at the little new cemetery:

Tend that flock of God whose shepherds you are, and do it, not under compulsion, but of your own free will , as God would have it; not for gain but out of sheer devotion; not tyrannizing over those who are allotted to your care, but setting an example to the flock. And then, when the Head Shepherd appears, you will receive for your own the unfading garland of glory.'

Now, looking back over the years, I think of that blessed, golden day on Arran as a time when God's Holy Spirit gently led me, giving me a sense of purpose when otherwise all would have seemed lost. The 'instructions' I received then: *While you still have a shadow, feed my sheep* I understood to mean: *While you still have life and breath, help other people.* Trying to put this into practice helped me to support Bob through the final stages of his illness, and then to face, with our children, the trauma of his death eight months later.

To this day, these 'instructions' continue to give me an aim in life. Indeed, that is why I have written this book....

• • •

Deo gratias

• • •

Acknowledgements

Apart from the two listed below, all Biblical quotations are from *The New English Bible*, Oxford and Cambridge University Presses, 1961, 1970.

(Chapter 1)   Copyright © Geoffrey Ashe 1968, taken from *Miracles*, Routledge & Kegan Paul. Reproduced by permission of the author c/o Rogers, Coleridge & White Ltd., 20 Powis Mews, London W11 1JN

(Chapter 3)   Richard Rodgers and Oscar Hammerstein, *South Pacific*, USA, Williamson Music Ltd., 1949.

(Chapter 5)   *The Penguin Book of German Verse*, Harmondsworth, Middlesex, 1959.

(Chapter 7)   *The Holy Bible*, King James' Version.

(Chapter 11)   *Trilingual New Testament*, USA, distributed in Europe by Gideons International. (UK base: Lutterworth, Leics.)

(Chapter 12)   Eric Crozier (text) and Benjamin Britten, Cantata: *St Nicholas*, Opus 42. © Copyright 1948 by Boosey & Co. Ltd., Reproduced by permission of Boosey & Hawkes Music Publishers Ltd..

(Chapter 16)   *Millennium Eyewitness*, complied by Brian Stone, London, Judy Piatkus (Publishers) Ltd., 1997.

My sincere thanks are due to the following:

to all members of my family for their constant love and support, especially my sister, Freda, and my children, Sally, Linda and Michael;

to Lynda Neilands and Iona Hicks, who edited my manuscript, for all their encouragement and help;

to Ronnie Russell, for his beautiful illustrations;

to John and Muriel Higgins, for their inspiring enthusiasm and expert advice;

and to all the friends who have encouraged me to publish my writing.

Postscript

It was early in 1997 that I first felt prompted to publish what had, up until then, been simply my own personal reminders of striking coincidences, noted in my diaries. At the induction of my church's young new minister, an inspiring sermon preached by his father had encouraged me to take the risk of 'going public'. At coffee time after the service, I had asked the preacher if he could recommend a publisher I might approach. He replied that he himself knew nothing of publishing, but gave me the name and telephone number of a relative of his who had had books published: a Mrs Elizabeth Urch.

Still fired with enthusiasm, I rushed home to phone her. Mrs Urch kindly discussed my project with me, then arranged to send me a copy of her book, *Be Still My Soul*, in which she describes how, as a young widow with three children, she coped after the death of her beloved husband. From that day on, I had - whenever my circumstances allowed - worked on my project, adding several new coincidences to those I had already selected, out of the many recorded over the twenty previous years. But because of my many other commitments, progress was slow, and eight years passed before I felt that my book was finally complete.

During the first three months of this year, 2005, I put everything else 'on hold', in order to have the manuscript ready for printing, before my daughter Linda and I set off on 10 April for a five-week visit to South Africa, Australia and Hong Kong. On 9 April, at the printers', I had the satisfying feeling that this project, started on the day I phoned Mrs Urch, had finally come to fruition.

When we boarded the London - Cape Town plane for the overnight flight, our stewardess said, 'I hope you don't mind, but I've changed your seating, so as to let a family sit together.' With us in the row of three was a lady whose seat had also been changed to accommodate the family. We all settled down to sleep as best we could.

In the morning, over breakfast, we began to chat. The lady told me that she was a nurse who had worked for 27 years in a Melbourne cancer hospital. She was on her way to Cape Town to visit a friend whom she had not seen for 30 years. On hearing my Scottish accent, she told me that she still kept in touch with a friend, Sheena, in Ayr, a former student at Edinburgh University. This turned out to be a former classmate of my sister Freda! As we began our descent into Cape Town, I asked her what her name was, so that I could tell Sheena that I had met her.

'Maureen Urch', she answered.

'That's an unusual name. You aren't by any chance related to a Mrs Elizabeth Urch who stays in Pitlochry?'

'She's my mother!' was the reply.